THE PASTONS

A Family in the
Wars of the Roses

THE PASTONS

A Family in the
Wars of the Roses

EDITED BY

RICHARD BARBER

THE BOYDELL PRESS

First published 1986
First published by The Boydell Press, Woodbridge 1993
Reprinted 1995, 1999

ISBN 0 85115 338 0

The Boydell Press is an imprint of Boydell & Brewer Ltd
PO Box 9, Woodbridge, Suffolk IP12 3DF, UK
and of Boydell & Brewer Inc.
PO Box 41026, Rochester NY 14604–4126, USA
website: http://www.boydell.co.uk

A catalogue record for this book is available
from the British Library

Library of Congress Catalog Card Number: 93–11789

This publication is printed on acid-free paper

Printed in Great Britain by
St Edmundsbury Press Ltd, Bury St Edmunds, Suffolk

INTRODUCTION

PRIVATE LETTERS WRITTEN IN ENGLISH WERE almost unknown before 1400. Those who could write would have used Latin or French, and the private letter in itself was unusual. Letters were for business, as compilers of medieval treatises made clear, though we do find a few examples of personal letters in an anonymous Italian work on the subject as early as 1135. The prime use of letters, according to another theorist, was as substitute for verbal instructions; if you could not actually speak to someone, it was best to send a letter because of 'the negligence of oral messengers and the [need for] concealment of secrets'. So letters were official instructions or reports, like the royal 'letters patent', open letters with the great seal attached to authenticate them, to be shown to all and sundry, or 'letters close', sealed up with the king's private seal. Apparently private letters, such as those written by members of the Black Prince's household while he was on campaign in France, were in fact meant for public consumption as newsletters, though private messages do appear: Sir John Wingfield, writing to Sir Richard Stafford with news on 22 January, 1356, reassures him that all his men are well and that he need not worry about them. Letters such as those of Peter Abelard and Heloise, which are indeed private, have a strong literary overtone; only people from their very cultured and learned background could have written them. Of course, official or exceptional letters were more likely to survive, and this distorts the picture to some extent; but it remains true to say that the private letter before 1400 was a rarity.

In the fifteenth century, the increase in general literacy and the emergence of a common language spoken by everyone from the king down to the humblest of his subjects meant that letters were much more widely used. If the recipient could not always read them, and the sender very often could not write them, there was always someone at hand to read them or to take dictation. None of the women of the Paston family appear to have written their own letters, while the men occasionally, but not often, did so: clerks were almost always used.

5

Furthermore, the value of written evidence was increasingly recognised in the law courts and in business, and letters could serve as a record. It was for this reason, rather than any sentimental or personal reason that letters were sent, read and kept. Almost every family of substance must have had its own archive; but of these only a handful have survived, even in part. Indeed, less than a dozen important groups have come down to us from the fifteenth century, and of these the most extensive are the Cely papers, from a London merchant family in the 1470s and 1480s, the Stonor papers from the Oxfordshire family of that name, and, best-known of all, the Paston letters.

Because the Paston letters form such a complete series, they are of considerable interest both to linguists and historians. The first modern edition by James Gairdner in 1872–5, revised in 1901, was based on the eighteenth century edition by John Fenn, and concentrated on the historical value of the letters. In recent years, Norman Davis has produced selections and most recently a definitive full edition primarily designed for linguists, in which the letters are grouped according to the member of the family who wrote them or to whom they were written, and careful attention is paid to the hand in which each letter is written; so that the autograph letters are clearly distinguished from those written to dictation by clerks. For the ordinary reader, these two editions are awkward to use, both because of the difficulties of fifteenth-century English and because the nature of the correspondence is such that a great deal of extra information is needed in order to understand the letters. Gairdner provided this in a lengthy introduction, which is difficult to relate to the letters themselves. At the time of writing, Davis' historical commentary has not yet appeared.

To a lesser degree, the same problems confront a reader in the modernised editions available, where the letters are presented in chronological order, with a varying amount of footnotes and introductory matters: even when the language is modernised, the turns of phrase are unfamiliar, and words have to be glossed because their meaning has changed, and footnotes can only sketch in a few details of the background. I have therefore adopted a radical approach, and have specifically excluded the reader who is interested in the Pastons' use of language. Such a reader can graduate from Norman Davis' excellent

World's Classics volume to the magisterial edition of the texts. What follows is designed for the reader who is interested in the content of the letters, and in following the fortunes of a family in the fifteenth century. Instead of a lengthy introduction, I have provided a continuous narrative framework, setting the letters in their context and, I hope, explaining the text by doing so. Letters are not always given in full, though omissions are generally indicated: again, the reader is referred to Davis' edition for the actual text. I have modernised both the spelling and the phraseology of the letters, excepting only the introductory and closing phrases of the letters, for which it is impossible to give a modern equivalent. The result is, I freely admit, a paraphrase of the originals; but if it helps to bring the Pastons and their world to life, it will have served its purpose.

A few general points about the historical commentary provided here need to be made. I have used the traditional terms 'Yorkist' and 'Lancastrian' for convenience, though modern historians tend, rightly, to avoid them. As the reader will quickly discover from the letters, the interplay of factions in this period was extremely complicated; even at a national level, three or four groups can be distinguished, with varying degrees of loyalty to their supposed party or king. At the local level, it was above all a matter of family interests, and a kaleidoscopic shifting and re-grouping of alliances was often the result. The three great magnates in the eastern counties during this period were the dukes of Norfolk and Suffolk and the earl of Oxford, and the relative strength or weakness of these men and their followers affected the Pastons far more than the larger movements on the national scene.

I am most grateful to Dr Roger Virgoe for reading the text and making most helpful suggestions: any errors or misinterpretations that remain are of course entirely my own.

RICHARD BARBER
November 1980

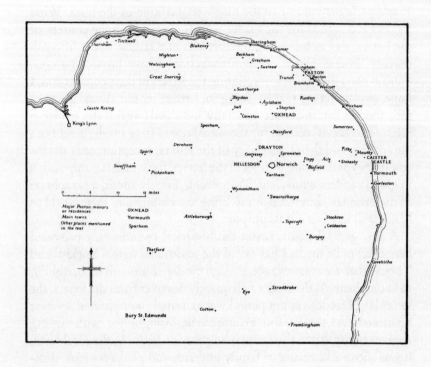

THE PASTONS

A Family in the
Wars of the Roses

GENEOLOGICAL TREE

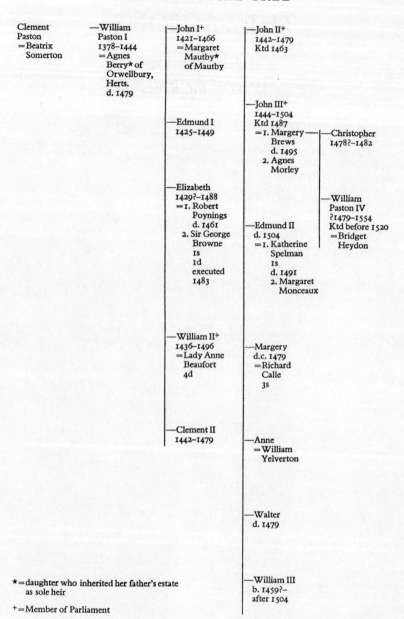

Clement
Paston
=Beatrix
  Somerton

—William
Paston I
1378–1444
=Agnes
  Berry★ of
  Orwellbury,
  Herts.
  d. 1479

—John I+
1421–1466
=Margaret
  Mautby★
  of Mautby

—Edmund I
1425–1449

—Elizabeth
1429?–1488
=1. Robert
  Poynings
  d. 1461
  2. Sir George
  Browne
  1s
  1d
  executed
  1483

—William II+
1436–1496
=Lady Anne
  Beaufort
  4d

—Clement II
1442–1479

—John II+
1442–1479
Ktd 1463

—John III+
1444–1504
Ktd 1487
=1. Margery
  Brews
  d. 1495
  2. Agnes
  Morley

—Edmund II
d. 1504
=1. Katherine
  Spelman
  1s
  d. 1491
  2. Margaret
  Monceaux

—Margery
d.c. 1479
=Richard
  Calle
  3s

—Anne
=William
  Yelverton

—Walter
d. 1479

—William III
b. 1459?–
after 1504

—Christopher
1478?–1482

—William
Paston IV
?1479–1554
Ktd before 1520
=Bridget
  Heydon

★=daughter who inherited her father's estate
  as sole heir

+=Member of Parliament

THE LITTLE VILLAGE OF PASTON lies on the Norfolk coast, just inland of that unbroken curving shore without true harbours or inlets that runs from Blakeney to Great Yarmouth. Paston is midway between the two, where the beach faces north-east towards Scandinavia, open to the bleak Arctic winds. Yet the village itself stands a mile or so inland, protected by the rise of the land, and open to the south and west. Like many villages, the old heart of the settlement has disappeared, and is marked only by the church, a great Tudor tithe-barn of 1581, and an eighteenth-century hall, on the site of the medieval mansion. The land is rich, and despite the unsightly north sea gas terminal just over the hill to seaward, this is still an agricultural community, remote enough in terms of modern England.

It was here that at the end of the fourteenth century there lived a certain Clement, who like his immediate forebears, used the name of the place he inhabited as a surname. A document drawn up in the 1450s by someone who was no friend of the family gives an account of his life-style, and how his son and grandson had improved the family fortunes:

A remembrance of the worshipful kin and ancestry of Paston,
born in Paston in the Soke of Gimingham.

'First there was one Clement Paston, dwelling in Paston, and he was a good plain husbandman, and lived on the land that he had in Paston, on which he kept a plough at all times of the year, and sometimes at the time for sowing barley two ploughs.

'The said Clement worked behind the plough both winter and summer, and he rode two miles bareback on horse with his corn under him, and brought home meal again under him. And he also drove his cart with various corn to Winterton to sell, as a good husbandman ought to do.

'Also, he had in Paston five score or six score acres of land at the most, and much of it was bond land of Gimingham Hall, with a poor little water-mill running by a little river there, or so it appears, in the old days.

'He had no other livelihood or manors, nor anything in any other place.

'And he wedded the sister of Geoffrey of Somerton, whose true surname is Goneld, who was a bondwoman; whose bondwoman she was is not known, if men will enquire. (She was in bond to the prior of Bromholm and Bacton as well, or so it is said.)

'And as for Geoffrey Somerton, he was a bondman also, to the same persons. He was both a pardoner and an attorney; and the world was good then, for he gathered many pence and half-pence, and with them he made a fair chapel at Somerton, so it appears.

'Also, the said Clement had a son, William, whom he sent to school; and he often borrowed the money to find his school fees; and after that he went to the courts with the help of his uncle Geoffrey Somerton, and learned the law, and did well for himself. Then he was made a serjeant, and afterwards a justice; he was a very knowledgeable man in law.

'And he purchased much land in Paston, and he also purchased half of the fifth part of the manor of Bacton called either Latimers or Stywards or Huntingfield, which half stretched into Paston. So with it and with another part of the said five parts he has lordship in Paston, but no manor place; and with this John Paston, son of the said William, wants to make himself a lordship there, to the great damage of the duke of Lancaster.

'And the said John desired to and has unjustly increased his estate by one tenant, as when the prior of Bromholm borrowed money from the said William to pay his tithes, the said William would not lend it him unless the said prior would mortgage to the said William one John Albon, the said prior's bondman, dwelling in Paston, who was a stubborn fellow and thrifty man, and would not obey the said William for that cause and because of the ill-will that the said William bore him, he desired him from the prior; and now after the death of the said William, the said John Albon died, and now John Paston, son to the said William, by force of the said mortgage, sent for the son of the said John Albon to Norwich.'

It is with William Paston, son of Clement Paston of Paston, that our story begins. Born in 1378, he was, as the writer of the anonymous account says, trained as a lawyer, the new way to success for an ambitious young man. In earlier times, the church would have been his only way out of the ties of the village, but the law was now an excellent alternative. He quickly made his mark, and gained a good local reputation: he acted as counsel for the city of Norwich in 1412–1415, and was in the service of the bishops of Norwich as well as being employed on royal business. In 1415, he became steward to the duke of Norfolk, and at the same time began a successful career in the royal courts, as a justice, becoming a justice of the Common Bench in 1429. In 1437 he was granted exemption for life from assizes outside his own area on account of his great age and the good service he had done under three kings as justice, serjeant-at-law and councillor-at-law of the duchy of Lancaster. He nonetheless continued to serve on commissions and as a justice until shortly before his death in 1444.

During his career as a lawyer, William Paston had been able to acquire substantial property. He married relatively late, in 1420, when he was forty-two; it was the year after his father died. His bride, who cannot have been much more than twenty-five and was probably about twenty years old, was Agnes Berry, daughter of a Hertfordshire knight, who inherited her father's lands on his death in 1433. William Paston gave her Oxnead in Norfolk, which he had recently bought, as her dowry; this manor, some ten miles south-west of Paston, was to be one of the family's principal residences in years to come.

William Paston's letters are business letters pure and simple. Some of the lawsuits in which he was concerned were not in defence of family property, but were undertaken on behalf of clients. The letter which follows is addressed to three monks and concerns a dispute over the priory of Bromholm, near Paston. William Paston was acting for Nicholas Loddon, who was installed as prior at Bromholm, against John Wortes, alias Paston, a distant relative of the family, who claimed to be the true prior. Prior Nicholas for his part accused Wortes of being an apostate. The outcome of this case is not clear, though it seems to have gone against Prior Nicholas; at any rate Paston was fined £205 by the Roman court and, when he tried to challenge the validity of the sentence, he was excommunicated.

1 March, 1426

'*Right worthy and worshipful sirs and master,* I commend myself to you and thank you with all my heart for the great tenderness you are pleased to have for the salvation of my simple honesty, praying you evermore of your good continuance. Following the advice of your letter, I have had the instrument duly examined by the wisest men I could find here, and especially by one Master Robert Sutton, a lawyer at the Roman court, who is my lord of Gloucester's chief and cherished man in his matter in the said court with my lady his wife. And their answer is that all this process of law, even if it were indeed carried out as the instrument specifies, is not sufficient in the law of the Holy Church; and that it seems to them, by the appearance of the instrument and from the defects that you saw in the same and in other papers, and in some manner by knowledge of the notary, that the process is for the most part false and untrue. I have taken advice of Master Robert Bruus, chancellor of my lord of Canterbury, and Master Nicholl Billesdon, chancellor with my lord of Canterbury, and Master John Blodwell, regarded as a learned man and a good lawyer at the said court; and all of them agree with the said Master Robert Sutton.

'Although I never heard any likely or credible evidence on this matter until I saw your letter and the instrument, yet I made an appeal and a procuration and an invocation at London long before Christmas by the advise of Master David Aprys, Master Symond Kempston and Master James Cole, and sent all this with instructions about the whole matter to my procurators at Rome by your brother the master subprior, and gave him gold to content him. And moreover, today I here and now make, as advised, a new appeal and new procuration; and about all this the said worthy men here say and inform me plainly that I have no reason, neither in law nor in conscience, to fear anything in this matter. My adversary has become bishop of Cork in Ireland, and there are two other persons still alive who were provided to the same bishopric before my adversary; and by accepting this bishopric he has deprived himself of the title that he claimed in Bromholm, and so annulled the grounds for his process against me. And also at the time of his pretended grievance and at the time of his suit, he was an apostate – and I believe he still is – and so unable to sue any such process.

'I intend to come home by London to learn more about this matter if I can. I pray that the Holy Trinity, lord of your church and of the world, may deliver me of my three adversaries – this cursed bishop over Bromholm, Aslak over Sprowston, and Juliana Heberd over Thornham. I have not trespassed against any of these three, God knows; yet I am foully and annoyingly vexed by them, to my great discomfort, and all for my lord's and friend's affairs and not for my own. I do not know whether it would be best, in some sermon or address in your church or elsewhere, to declare anything of this matter in order to stop the rumours about the case. I submit myself and the whole affair to your good discretion, and always thank God and yourselves, who keep both you and me in his gracious governance.

'I expect to see you on Palm Sunday. Written at Leicester, Friday of the third week of Lent.

'All the said learned men tell me that there is truly neither danger nor difficulty for anyone in taking down the instrument and bill, which I send back to you by the bearer of this, asking you to keep it as private as you can. I have asked my master Hammond to send you news and gossip.'

Your man, W. Paston

Of Paston's other two 'great adversaries' we know little about the case at Thornham brought by Juliana Heberd except for petitions from her alleging wrongful imprisonment; but a lawsuit with Walter Aslak is documented. It does not directly concern Sprowston, but arose out of an attempt to discredit William Paston which was part and parcel of the same affair. What survives is the two documents which were presented to arbitrators, headed by the duke of Norfolk, in June 1428. They tell a story of a deep-seated quarrel, in which each side seems to have given as good as they got. Paston's version begins with a tale of riot and disorder on the night of 31 December, 1423 when

'certain unknown malefactors, felons and breakers of the king's peace, estimated at eighty or more in number, with malice and imagination aforethought, feloniously broke into the dwelling-place of John Grys of Wighton in Wighton in the shire of Norfolk, and hewed down the gates and doors of the said place with carpenters' axes. They took John Grys, his son, and a serving-man of theirs, and led them to a pair of gallows a mile from the said dwelling place, in order to hang them there. But because they had no rope to hand for their felonous purpose, they slew and murdered the said John Grys, his son, and his man in the most horrible fashion ever heard of in that country. Whereupon Walter Aslak, intending and imagining that he would put William Paston in dread and intolerable fear of being slain and murdered in the same way, by force and against the king's peace. . . posted certain English bills, partly in rhyme, on the gates of Trinity Priory Church and the Minorite Church in Norfolk, and in the city gates called Needham and Westwick gates, doing this in his own person and by Richard Killingworth, at that time his servant. These bills threatened the said William Paston with such and so many menaces of death and dismemberment, mentioning and implying that the said William and his clerks and servants should be slain and murdered in the same way as the said John Grys had been murdered, and they also contained these two words in Latin, "et cetera", by which it was generally understood that those who had made the bills intended more malice and harm to the said William, his clerks and servants, than was set out in the said bills. . .'

William Paston claimed that the bills had the effect desired by those who posted them up, and that he and his servants 'durst not walk and ride in freedom'. A lawsuit followed, in which Paston was awarded £120 for trespass; but Aslak refused to pay, and was imprisoned as a result. Aslak pursued a counter-claim against Paston, which the latter claimed was false, and continued to menace him. William Paston concludes that the only reason for Aslak's behaviour is that he had been the losing party in a lawsuit over the advowson of Sprowston Church, in which William Paston had successfully defended the prior of Norwich's title to it.

Aslak's evidence is rather different. He claimed that he had nothing to do with the bills, which were entirely the work of Richard Killingworth, and that Paston had used trickery to get a verdict against him in the court, and, despite a previous undertaking that he would not have him imprisoned, had him put in gaol when he failed to pay the damages. All in all, it seems a fairly unsavoury affair. Aslak may have been responsible for the threats, as it seems he was; but Paston did not stop at using every kind of legal tactic to get the better of his enemy. As Sir Thomas Erpingham rightly said in an early stage of the affair, 'you cannot show any bodily harm, but only defamation of your name', and this was not a matter for criminal law: yet Aslak undoubtedly spent a considerable time in prison as a result of Paston's manoeuvres, even though Paston professed himself unwilling even to secure writs of distraint to get his money. Juliana Heberd's petition tells a not dissimilar tale of imprisonments on technical grounds, and however brilliant a lawyer Paston may have been, it seems that he was ruthless in dealing with his opponents. Yet his reputation generally was that of a good and honest lawyer; admittedly in 1433 a petition was presented to parliament accusing him of taking bribes, but nothing came of it, and it certainly did not damage Paston's subsequent career.

William Paston died in 1444. It is only after his death that the letters really begin to come alive. They reflect the attempts of his wife and heirs to hold onto the estates which they had inherited from him in the face of determined attacks on this upstart family. We have just one surviving note from Agnes Paston to her husband, when she was negotiating a match for her eldest son John with Margaret Mautby, daughter of John Mautby of Mautby near Caister, an heiress of some substance. This was an arranged match, designed to further the family's fortunes, but William Paston was elsewhere on business when the couple first met and was clearly anxious to know how matters were going. Agnes Paston was able to reassure him:

20 April, 1440 [?]

'*Dear husband*, I commend myself to you, etc. Blessed be God, I send you good tidings of the coming and bringing home of the gentlewoman whom you know of from Reedham tonight, according to the appointment that you yourself made. And as for the first acquaintance between John Paston and the said gentlewoman, she gave him a gentle welcome in gentle fashion and said he was indeed your son.

17

And so I hope that no great negotiations will be needed between them.

'The parson of Stockton told me that if you would buy her a gown, her mother would give a good fur to trim it. The gown needs to be bought, and the colour ought to be a good blue or else a bright blood-red.

'Please buy me two reels of gold thread. Your fish ponds are doing well.

'The Holy Trinity keep you in their care. Written at Paston in haste on the Wednesday after the third Sunday after Easter, for lack of a good secretary, etc.'

Yours, Agnes Paston

The marriage took place during the summer or early autumn, John still being an undergraduate at Peterhouse in Cambridge. It was to Peterhouse that Margaret addressed her first surviving letter to him some time soon after their marriage, a fairly businesslike note mainly concerned with local news:

'*Right reverend and worshipful husband*, I commend myself to you with all my simple heart. This is to let you know that 1100 Flemish landed at Waxham, of whom 800 were captured, killed or drowned. If they had not been, you would have been at home this Whitsuntide, and I expect that you will be at home before very long.

'I thank you for your letter, for I had none from you since I last spoke with you about the business of John Marriott. The inquest did not take place today, for my lord of Norfolk was in town for Wetherby's case; and for that reason he would not let it take place. As far as I know, neither Finch nor Kilby are scheming to do him any good.

'I write no more to you this time, but the Holy Trinity have you in their keeping.

'Written at Norwich on Trinity Sunday.'

Your Margaret Paston

None of John Paston's early letters to Margaret survive, but later in the same year, they were once again separated, and Margaret wrote to him in rather more intimate terms:

14 [?] December, 1441

'*Right reverend and worshipful husband*, I commend myself to you,

18

desiring heartily to hear of your welfare, thanking you for the token that you sent me by Edmund Perys. Please let me tell you that my mother sent to my father in London for some grey woollen gown cloth, to make me a gown, and he told my mother and me when he came home that he had instructed you to buy it after you left London. If it is not yet bought, please be so kind as to buy it and send it home as soon as you can, for I have no gown to wear this winter except my black and green one with tapes, and that is so cumbersome that I am tired of wearing it.

'As to the girdle that my father promised me, I spoke to him about it a little while before he last went to London, and he said to me that it was your fault, because you would not think about having it made: but I expect that it is not so – he said it just as an excuse. I ask you, if you dare take it upon you, to be so good as to have it made in time for your return home, for I never needed it more than I do now, for I have grown so fat that no belt or girdle that I have will go round me.

'Elisabeth Peverel has lain sick for fifteen or sixteen weeks with sciatica, but she sent my mother word by Kate that she would come here when God sent time, even if she had to be wheeled in a barrow.

'John Damme was here, and my mother revealed my secret to him and he said by his troth that he was not so pleased by anything he had heard for the last twelve months as he was by that news. I can no longer live by cunning; my secret is revealed to everyone who sees me. I sent you word of all the other things that you desired me to send word of in a letter I wrote on Our Lady's day last [8 December].

'The Holy Trinity have you in their keeping. Written at Oxnead in very great haste on the Thursday before St Thomas' day.

'Please wear the ring with the image of St Margaret that I sent you as a keepsake until you come home. You have left me such a keepsake as makes me think of you both day and night when I want to sleep.'

Yours, M.P.

Two other letters in similar vein survive from 1443–4; they are almost entirely personal, and are quite different from the predominantly business-like missives of later years. John was still studying at the Inner Temple, as a gentleman of leisure, and the news passed between them was mostly gossip, though the first letter begins on a more serious note. Margaret was living with her mother-in-law at Oxnead, while her own mother was living at Geldeston near Beccles with her second husband, Ralph Garneys.

28 September, 1443

'*Right worshipful husband*, I commend myself to you, desiring with all my heart to hear how you are and thanking God for your recovery from the great illness you have had; and I thank you for the letter you sent me, for I swear that my mother-in-law and I were not easy in our hearts from the time that we knew of your sickness until we knew for certain of your recovery. My mother-in-law has promised another image of wax weighing as much as you for our lady of Walsingham, and she sent four nobles (26s 8d) to the four orders of friars in Norwich to pray for you. I have promised to go on a pilgrimage to Walsingham and St Leonard's Priory (in Norwich) for you. By my troth, I have never had such a weary time as I had from the time that I knew of your sickness to the time I knew of your recovery, and even now I am not very much at ease, nor shall I be until I know that you are completely better.

'Your father and mine was at Beccles a week ago today on the prior of Bromholm's business, and he stayed at Geldeston that night; he was there until nine o'clock the next day. And I sent a message asking for a gown from there, and my mother said that I could not have one until I went there again; and so they could not get one. My stepfather Garneys sent word that he would be here next week, and my aunt too, and would have some sport with their hawks; and they want to take me home with them. And, so God help me, I shall make an excuse for not going there, if I can, because I expect that I shall get news from you here more easily than I would have there.

'I shall send my mother a token that she gave me, for I suppose the time has come to send it to her if I am to keep the promise that I have made – I think that I have told you what it was. I beg you with all my heart to be kind and send me a letter as quickly as you can, if writing is

not difficult for you, and that you will send me word how your sore is.
If I could have had my way, I would have seen you before now. I wish
you were at home, if you would have been more comfortable here,
and your sore might have been as well looked after here as it is where
you are now; I would rather have you here than be given a new gown,
even though it was a scarlet one. Please, if your sore is healed and you
can bear to ride, when my father comes to London, ask him for leave
and come home when the horses are sent home again, for I think you
will be looked after as tenderly here as you are in London.

'I cannot find time to write half a quarter as much as I would tell you
if I could speak to you. I shall send you another letter as soon as I can. I
shall be grateful if you can remember my girdle, and if you can write
to me now, because I expect writing has been difficult for you. Almighty God have you in his keeping and send you health. Written at
Oxnead in very great haste on St Michael's eve.

Yours, M. Paston

'My mother-in-law sends you greetings and God's blessing and hers,
and asks you, as I do also, to keep to a good diet of meat and drink, for
that will do more than anything to help you to recover. Your son is
well, blessed be God.'

Geldeston, 8 July, 1444

'*Right reverend and worshipful husband*, I commend myself to you,
desiring with all my heart to hear that you are well, and thanking you
for your letter and for the things that you sent me with it. And as for
John Estegate, he has neither come nor sent anything here yet, so I
expect I shall have to borrow money soon if you do not come home
soon, because I do not think I shall get any from him. God help me, I
have only 4s, and I owe almost as much money as comes to that
amount.

'I have done your errands to your mother and my uncle, and as for
the trustees of Stokesby, my uncle says that there are no more than he
wrote to you about that he knows of. And I have also delivered the
other thing that you sent me sealed in the box as you ordered me to,
and the man I delivered it to says that he wants nothing of the deal except such things as were done before he came there, which you told

him about. He says he would not want to be troubled with any such thing as that is, or to have it done in his time, for twenty marks. I expect he will let you know shortly what he will do.

'Please be kind enough to buy me some lace like that enclosed as samples in this letter, and one piece of black lace. As for the caps you sent me for the children, they are too small for them. Pease buy finer and bigger caps than those. Please remember me to my father- and mother-in-law, and tell them that all their children are well, blessed be God.

'Heydon's wife had her child on Saint Peter's day. I have heard since that her husband wants nothing to do with her, nor with the child she has just had either. I heard it said that he said that if she came into his presence to make her excuse, he would cut off her nose so that everyone would know what she was, and if the child came into his presence, he would kill it. He will not be persuaded to have her back on any account, so I hear.

'The Holy Trinity have you in their keeping and send you health. Written at Geldeston on Wednesday after St Thomas's day.'

By yours, M. Paston

A little over a month after this was written, William Paston died, on 13 August. He had been unwell at intervals for some years; in January 1444 he was unable to ride because of sciatica. At sixty-six he was an elderly man by the standards of the time, so his death was not entirely unexpected. But it left his widow with a young family and wide estate to manage. John had now finished his education, but Edmund was still at Clements Inn, and the two youngest sons were eight and two respectively. John and Edmund were at once involved in business matters, and Margaret too, was soon writing a very different kind of letter to her husband. Nor was the inheritance an undisputed one. Twenty years later, Agnes remembered when drafting her own will how John had quarrelled with her over the disposal of William's lands, seizing lands which, although not specifically allocated in his will, had been intended – or so she said – for John's younger brothers, and removing money deposited at Norwich Priory by William so that the other executors could not regain it. Echoes of this family quarrel were to continue for many years, but for the moment there were more serious threats to the inheritance from outsiders.

The family had to make good their claim to William's estates without any of his influence at court or at law, and it was not long before old jealousies and resentments suppressed during William's lifetime, began to break out. Within six months of his death, Agnes had disturbing news to report to Edmund in London:

4 February, 1445

'*To my well-beloved son.* I greet you well, and advise you to think once a day of your father's counsel to learn the law; for he said many times that whoever lived at Paston would need to know how to defend himself.

'The vicar of Paston and your father came to a thorough agreement last Lent, and stakes were set up to show how broad the highway should be; and now he has pulled up the stakes, and says he wants to make a ditch from the corner of his wall right across the highway to the new ditch of the large enclosure. And there is also a man in Trunch called Palmer, who had some land in Trunch from your father seven or eight years ago for rent to be paid in corn, and has paid regularly every year; and now he has allowed the corn to be seized in payment of 8s in rent to Gimingham [manor], which your father never paid. Geoffrey asked Palmer why the rent was not demanded in my husband's time, and Palmer said it was because he was a great man, and skilled in law, and that was why men would not demand the rent. I am sending you the names of the men that filled in the pit that was in Gynnis Close written on a note enclosed in this letter.

'I am not sending you this letter to make you weary of Paston, for I live in hope; and you will learn that they shall be made weary of their work, for in good faith I can tell you that it was your father's last will to have done right well for that place; and I can show good proof of it, even if men would deny it.

'God make you truly a good man, and send you God's blessing and mine. Written in haste at Norwich the Thursday after Candlemas day.

'Find out from your brother John how many joists are needed for the parlour and chapel at Paston, and what length, breadth and thickness they must be; for your father's wish was, so I believe, that they should be nine inches one way and seven the other. So arrange that they may be squared up there and sent here, for here in this part of the country there are none such to be had. And say to your brother John that it would be as well to think about Stansted Church. And I pray you to send me news from overseas, for here they are afraid to say what has been reported.'

From your mother, Agnes Paston

The vicar seems to have been clearly in the wrong, for Paston had obtained a patent from the king to divert the highway, and the diversion was only a small one. But the temper of the times was changing. In 1437, the sixteen-year-old king, Henry VI, had declared his minority to be at an end, and had taken over the government himself. The regency council which had ruled England since 1422 had provided stable government and had prevented rivalries among the great nobles from becoming open feuds. There was, it is true, a high degree of lawlessness, and there was dissatisfaction over the long drawn out and costly wars in France. Henry's accession to power made matters worse rather than better. He was far from being a forceful character like his father and grandfather; peace-loving, religious and easily persuaded, he was unable to control the great magnates and all too ready to give offices and power to his friends and flatterers, who thus had an entrenched interest in seeing that he was firmly under their own control. Patronage became everything. William Paston had shrewdly foreseen this and had placed John Paston in the duke of Norfolk's household; but his son was not as skilful at making his way in this world of intrigues and favour-seeking as he might have been, and the family's relations with the duke were at best ambiguous: they certainly could not count on his favour as a certainty. The letters that survive suggest that the duke regarded John Paston as someone on whom he could rely for help over an election or as part of his retinue on a ceremonial occasion, but not as a close confidant. In 1443, John Paston had acted for the duke over a disputed inheritance, but this was the nearest he came to doing any special service for him.

If the Pastons had few friends in high places, they had dangerous enemies with support from great magnates. In the next surviving letter, from Edmund Paston to his elder brother, the shadow of these factions looms even larger than before.

5 July, 1447 [?]

'*Right worshipful brother*, I commend myself to you. Please write to my mother on your own account to advise her to keep matters to herself and not to tell anybody anything of her intentions, for she will tell many people of her intentions one day and the next day she will swear that the same men are false. I have seen part of the evidence, and the manor [Oxnead] was purchased piecemeal, and certain enfeoffments made of the advowson and some pieces of land, leaving the manor, and I know well that you have a collateral release with the warranty of one of Hauteyn's wives for the whole manor.

'Steward, the chief constable, told me he was empanelled on the assize between you and Frances. He asked my advice as to what he should do about it, because he said it was taken in Sir Thomas Tuddenham's name. He would be glad to be challenged. I advised him to swear the truth of the issue to which he would be sworn, and then he would never need to fear any charge of giving a false verdict. I gave him this advice and no other. He enquired about the influence of Thomas Daniel and the marquis of Suffolk, and asked me which of them I thought would rule in this shire, and I said both, so I believe; and he who survives will hold by virtue of surviving, and will thank his friends and settle with his enemies. I feel that he wants to forsake his master and get a new one, if he was sure who would rule. And I think that many in the country are inclined in the same way.

'The Holy Trinity keep you. Written at Norwich on the Wednesday after St Peter's day.'

Your brother, E. Paston

As Edmund's letter indicates, trouble had arisen over another part of William Paston's property. This time it was the manor of Oxnead, which he had given to Agnes as long ago as 1420 as her dowry. Paston had bought it with a good title, or so it seemed to the experienced lawyer: but a member of the family that had once owned it now appeared and entered a claim. He was John Hauteyn, a Carmelite friar, who, as a member of that order, was debarred from holding property. However, he got round this difficulty by claiming that he had been forced into the order while under age, and obtained a dispensation from his vows from the Pope. William Paston had got word of this, and had drawn up a memorandum to show that Hauteyn was lying and had entered the order of his own free will when he was fourteen. Hauteyn nonetheless took the case to court after William Paston's death, though he petitioned the archbishop of Canterbury for help in getting lawyers.

'. . . John Hauteyn, chaplain, meekly beseeches your lordship that whereas he has various suits and actions at law to be sued against Agnes who was the wife of W. Paston of the manor of Oxnead in the county of Norfolk, and forasmuch as your said beseecher can get no counsel among lawyers to act for him in the said matter because the said William Paston was one of the king's justices, and John Paston, son and heir to the said William Paston is also a man of the lawcourts, it will please your lordship to assign [counsel to act for him] in the said cases and others that he has against the said Agnes and others.'

Hauteyn had friends in high places who were prepared to use other methods, however: early in 1449 one of the family retainers, James Gresham, who had been William Paston's clerk, wrote to John Paston:

'*Worthy and worshipful Sir and my right good master*, I commend myself to you, and let you know that I had supper with my mistress your wife at Mrs Clere's, and, blessed be God, they are well and hope that you will send them good news of your case when you know for certain what the result is. My mistress your mother came there; and she is well, and sends you God's blessing and hers, and she told me to write to you to say that she has genuine information from a true and trustworthy man, whose name she will tell you herself when you next meet, that there was a plot for a great crowd, from a remarkable gathering of sailors near Covehithe, to come to Oxnead and to eject her in worse fashion than you were ejected from Gresham. And they planned to go to Oxnead and to have looted it and put the priest in there; but their plan was not carried out, because they were countermanded, though how this happened I cannot yet discover. And she has been told that they planned to be at Oxnead about mid-Lent and I have been promised two days' warning by a good friend. So she asks you to watch carefully whether the priest comes into this part of the world or not; for if anything is done I think the friar will be there at the doing of it. And if you find out that he is coming here, send my mistress word as quickly as you can, with your advice and anything else necessary.

'And God have you in his keeping. Written at nine o'clock on Monday evening before St Gregory's day in haste. My brother Beck and his fellows will tell you more than I can write now.'

Your servant, J. Gresham

That summer, Agnes Paston reported that the friar had been 'at St Benet's and Norwich, and boasted greatly of the case he had against us, and bought many boxes, though I do not know why. It would be as well to watch out in London in case he brings an assize case about St Margaret's day [20 July]'. Hauteyn did make one attempt to gain possession, though the memorandum which describes his appearance at Oxnead is undated. The episode cannot be later than mid-March 1449, because Edmund Paston died in London about March 21; it could easily belong to the previous year. The note was written by James Gloys, Agnes Paston's chaplain and adviser:

'Today at ten o'clock Edmund Paston and the parson of Oxnead went out of the manor down to Wantown Gap, for they heard news that the friar was coming; and with the friar came John Cates and one Walter Herman of Wheytte and William Yemmys of Burgh and the friar's man. And Edmund Paston said to John Cates, "Welcome", and he asked them what their reason for coming was. The friar said he came to speak with the good lady [i.e. Agnes Paston], and Edmund said that he could not speak to her at this time; she was so occupied that he could not speak with her. And he said that he would try, and so rode on from Wantown Gap to the great gate; and there he alighted and knocked on the gate, and we followed as quickly as we could. And John Joallere and John Edmunds were inside and asked the friar what he wanted; and he said that he wanted to come in and speak to the good lady of the house, and they said no, he could not come in. And then Edmund Paston and the parson came up, and asked him the reason for coming at this time; and he said it was to enter into the manor of Oxnead, which his father had possessed, and his ancestors from King Edward the Third until Colby's time, and that he had found an entail of it in the royal records. And then Edmund Paston replied to him, and said that it would be best for him to declare his evidence in Westminster Hall: and he answered that he would do so when he could.

'And he said to those that came with him, "Sirs, I charge you to bear witness how I am kept out by force and may not take possession." And at the same instant he pushed towards the gate in order to lay hands on it, and then the said Edmund removed him from the gate, saying "But for respect for your lord and mine, I would see your heart's blood or you should see mine before you lay hand on the gate." And then the said friar said scornfully that he might thank his master, and the said Edmund answered that he might indeed thank his lord. Then he bent down and picked up some earth and gave it to his man, saying to those that came with him: "I charge you all in the king's behalf that you bear witness that I hereby take possession of my inheritance." Edmund said that this taking of possession was invalid, and then the friar said that since he might not have it now, he would come again another time.

'Edmund has ridden off to Heydon. We were told this afternoon that three men came from Skeyton and met the friar in the fields and spoke him for a good while, and then rode off the same way as they came.'

Early the following month it was Margaret Paston's turn to report on the friar's doings.

2 April, 1449

'The friar who claims Oxnead was in this town yesterday and today, and was staying at Bury's house; and this afternoon he rode off, but I do not know where to. He said openly in this town that he would get Oxnead and that he has the protection of my lord of Suffolk, who would look after him in the affair. In the last two days, somebody warned my mother-in-law to beware, saying plainly that she would get the same treatment as she had at Gresham within a very short time.'

However, the friar's case ended, not with violence, but with a lawsuit. As William Paston had foreseen, the lawsuit hinged on the validity of Hauteyn's claim to be released from his vows, and John Paston made moves to get papers from Rome annulling the dispensation. But the case fades out of the correspondence after 1450, and a compromise seems to have been reached at some time during that year. Greater events had overtaken Hauteyn. His 'claim' relied largely on the protection of the duke of Suffolk, but early in 1450 the smouldering discontent with Henry VI's government came to a head. Suffolk, as the king's chief minister was the target of resentment, and in February he was formally impeached by the Commons. A copy of the articles of impeachment was kept by the Pastons among their papers, doubtless because they had a keen interest in the approaching downfall of the man who seemed to be their chief enemy. Early in March, Suffolk was brought before the Lords; he denied the charges, but no formal trial took place, since Henry took the matter into his own hands, and sentenced Suffolk to five years' banishment. Suffolk left Ipswich at the end of April. John Paston learned what happened next a day or two later.

'*Right worshipful Sir*, I commend myself to you, and am very sorry to have to tell you what follows; I have so washed this little note with sorrowful tears that you will hardly be able to read it. On the Monday after May Day, news came to London that, on the Thursday before, the duke of Suffolk came to the Kentish coast near Dover with his two ships and a little pinnace, which he sent with certain letters by certain of his trusted men to Calais, to find out how he would be received there. And a ship called *Nicholas of the Tower*, escorted by other ships, met the pinnace, and the master of the *Nicholas* learned from those in the pinnace that the duke was coming. And when he saw the duke's ships he sent his boat to find out who they were, and the duke himself spoke to them and said that he was sent to Calais by the king's orders. And they said he must speak to their master; and so he, with two or three of his men, went with them in their boat to the *Nicholas*. And when he arrived, the master greeted him with "Welcome, traitor" or so men say; and furthermore the master asked the sailors if they would support the duke, and they sent word that they would in no way do so.

'Some say that he wrote from there several times asking to be handed over to the king, but that is not known for certain. He had his confessor with him. And some say that he was tried on the ship, after the sailors' fashion, on the impeachment, and found guilty.

'Also he asked the name of the ship, and when he knew it he remembered Stacey, who said that if he could escape the danger of the tower, he would be safe: and then his heart failed him, for he thought he had been deceived. And in everyone's sight he was taken out of the great ship into the boat: and there was an axe and a block there. One of the roughest men on the ship told him to lay his head on it, and he would be fairly dealt with and die by the sword; and he took a rusty sword, and cut off his head with half a dozen strokes, and took off his russet gown and his doublet of velvet covered with metal plates and laid his body on the sands of Dover. And some say his head was set up on a pole by it, and his men set on shore after much pleading and prayer. And the sheriff of Kent is keeping watch on the body, and sent his under-sheriff to the judges to know what to do, and also to the king. What else will be done I do not know; but this is what has happened so far; if the procedure be wrong, let his [i.e. Suffolk's] learned counsel reverse it!

'As for all your other affairs, they sleep, and the friar too.

'Written in great haste at London the fifth day of May, by your servant.'

W[illiam] L[omnor]

Even though the Pastons and their followers had no cause to love Suffolk, the tragic end of the duke provoked their shocked sympathy as a first reaction. It was for the chroniclers, mulling over events at leisure, to see his death as the just punishment of a tyrant; for the ordinary man, the spectacle of such a fall, in a society where order was sacrosanct, was both dreadful and disturbing. On reflection, however, the Pastons must have found Suffolk's death a relief, for this was very probably the reason for Hauteyn's abandonment of his action.

They had other problems on their hands, however, as is implied by the references to events at Gresham in the letters already quoted. This was another of William Paston's purchases, the previous owner being Thomas Chaucer, son of the poet Geoffrey Chaucer. Thomas Chaucer had acquired half the manor of Gresham by marriage, and bought the reversion (i.e. eventual title) to the other half, which later came into his possession as well. One of the Moleyns family had had an option to buy this reversion, but failed to exercise it. However, after William Paston's death, a claimant appeared in the shape of Lord Hungerford's son, who had married into the Moleyns family, and had become a peer with the title of Lord Moleyns. He was attempting to secure the whole Moleyns inheritance, but his claim to Gresham was weak in the extreme. If it had not been for the influence of a local lawyer, John Heydon, and his crony, Sir Thomas Tuddenham, both of them creatures of the duke of Suffolk, Moleyns would probably have let matters be. With their advice, however, he made his claim, not in the courts, but by force, seizing the manor on February 17, 1448. John Paston, realising the strength of his opponents, pursued the matter as best he could, by appealing to Moleyns himself. However, the general situation in Norfolk was growing daily more difficult, and Margaret Paston reported that spring that there had been trouble from John Wymondham, one of Heydon and Tuddenham's allies, a quarrel which was not related to the disputes over Gresham, but arose out of pure factional rivalry:

19 May, 1448

'*Right worshipful husband*, I commend myself to you. This is to let you know last Friday before noon, while the parson of Oxnead was at mass in our parish church [in Norwich], before the elevation of the Host, James Gloys, who had been in the town, came home by Wymondham's gate. Wymondham was standing in his gateway, with John Norwood, his man, by him, and Thomas Hawes, his other man, stood in the street by the side of the street drain. And James Gloys came with his hat on his head between both his men. And when Gloys was opposite Wymondham, Wymondham said: "Uncover thy head!" and Gloys replied "So I will, for thou!"* And when Gloys was three or

* The use of 'thou' instead of the formal 'you' would have been an insult.

31

four paces past him, Wymondham drew out his dagger and said "Wilt thou, knave?" And at that Gloys turned and drew his dagger and defended himself, fleeing into my mother's place; and Wymondham and his man Hawes threw stones and drove Gloys into my mother's place. And Hawes followed him into my mother's and threw a stone as big as a farthing loaf into the hall after Gloys, and then ran out of the place again. And Gloys followed him out and stood outside the gate; then Wymondham called Gloys a thief and said he would kill him, and Gloys said he lied and called him a churl, and told him to come on himself or send the best man he had, and Gloys would match him, one against one. And then Hawes ran into Wymondham's place and fetched a spear and a sword, and took his master his sword. With the noise of this affray and assault my mother and I came out of the church at the consecration, and I told Gloys to go back into my mother's place; and he did so.

'And then Wymondham called my mother and myself strong whores, and said the Pastons and all their family were [*lacuna*] said he lied, knave and churl that he was. And he used much strong language, as I will tell you later.

'In the afternoon, my mother and I went to the prior of Norwich and told him the whole incident, and the prior sent for Wymondham. We went home again, and Pagrave came home with us. And while Wymondham was with the prior, Gloys was standing in the street at my mother's gate, and Hawes saw him there as he stood in Lady Hastings' [Wymondham's wife's] chamber. Soon he came down again with a two-handed sword and assaulted Gloys again, and Thomas my mother's man. He let fly a blow at Thomas, and grazed his hand with his sword. As for this later assault, the parson of Oxnead saw it and will vouch for it. And much else was done, as Gloys will tell you. And because of the dangers that might ensue from all this, on my mother's advice and that of the others I am sending you Gloys to be with you for a time, for my own peace of mind. In good faith, I would not have such trouble again for forty pounds.

'. . . The Lord Moleyns' man is collecting the rent at Gresham very quickly, and James Gresham will tell you more fully about it when he comes.

'No more at this time, but Almighty God have you in his keeping. Written in haste on Trinity Sunday at evening.'

Yours, Margaret Paston

John Paston pursued his cause with Moleyns all summer, but seeing that he was making no progress, he decided to make his presence felt in Gresham and on October 6, he 'inhabited a mansion within the said town'. It was clear that there would soon be trouble, and while he was away on business, Margaret was left in charge, and found herself facing what looked like an imminent siege:

1448

'*Right worshipful husband*, I commend myself to you and ask you to get some crossbows, and windlasses to wind them with, and crossbow bolts, for your houses here are so low that no one can shoot out of them with a longbow, however much we needed to. I expect you can get such things from Sir John Fastolf if you were to send to him. And I would also like you to get two or three short pole-axes to keep indoors, and as many leather jackets, if you can.

'Partridge [Moleyns' bailiff] and his companions are very much afraid that you will try to reclaim possession from them, and have made great defences within the house, so I am told. They have made bars to bar the doors crosswise, and loopholes at every corner of the house out of which to shoot, both with bows and hand-guns; and the holes that have been made for hand-guns are barely knee high from the floor, and five such holes have been made. No one could shoot out from them with hand bows.

'Purry made friends with William Hasard at Querles' house and told him that he would come and drink with Partridge and him; and he said he would be welcome. That afternoon he went there to see what they did and what company they had with them. When he came there the doors were bolted fast and there was no one with them but Margaret and Capron and his wife and Querles' wife, and another man in black, who walked with a limp; I think from what he said that it was Norfolk of Gimingham. And Purry saw all this, and Marriott and his company boasted greatly; but I will tell you about that when you come home.

'Please be so kind as to buy me a pound of almonds, a pound of sugar, and buy some frieze-cloth to make gowns for your children. You will get the cheapest and the best choice from Hay's wife, I am told.

'Please buy a yard of black broadcloth for a hood for me, at 3s 8d or 4s a yard, for there is neither good cloth nor frieze in this town. As for the children's gowns, if I have cloth I will have them made. The Trinity have you in their keeping and send you good fortune in all your affairs.'

The state of affairs at Gresham was also reported by John Damme, the recorder of Norwich and an MP, who was a trusted friend of the Pastons. He wrote to John Paston in London:

30 November, 1448

'May it please your good mastership to know that my mistress your wife commends herself to you and is well, blessed be God; and all your following are well and commend themselves to you. I was with my lord of Oxford, and did my errand; and I found his good lordship well disposed towards you, for he said that if he was sent for to come, he would not be slow if it were good weather, and if it rained he would come all the same.

'Furthermore I spoke with Partridge about the letter sent to my Lord Moleyns. He says that he knew that it had been written, and can produce twenty witnesses, but he would give me no names; so he and I were unable to come to a full agreement. And I told him to remember that he could not stay there if you wanted to eject him; and he said that he knew that well, but if you ejected him, you yourself would be ejected again soon afterwards. And I said that if this was the case, they would not stay there long. And Marriott stood by and said that would not be surprising while there were only two of them there, but it would not be the best thing to do and I said that I was telling them that it would be so if you wished it, even if they gathered all the forces that they could. And Marriott said loftily that it could not be carried out; and there were more words, too long to write at the moment. Partridge and his companion are putting a bold face on things, and hold great feasts and dinners, saying that my Lord Moleyns has written openly to them that he is lord there, and will be and shall be,

34

and you are not to have the place; but I trust in God's righteousness for a better outcome. Please remember what Heydon is doing and can do as a justice of the peace, being an adviser of my lord and no good friend or well-wisher of yours; and confer with your advisers as to what you must put up with by law, and what you can do to resist.

'On Sunday last, Gunore and Marriott and John Davy dined with Partridge; and after evensong Gunore spoke to my mistress and told her to get her men to lay aside their battle-axes and leather jackets; and she replied that they had no intention of trying to hurt anyone, but it was said that she was to be thrown out of her house, and she was reluctant to let that happen. So she said that they should go armed until you came home. And he said loftily that unless they put down their arms and armour it would be taken off them. I hope he has a better warrant than his proud language, or he will not find it easy to get them from them.

'All this I send to you to remember well, with God's help, to whom I pray to guide you aright to his worship and your heart's desire. Written at Sustead on St Andrew's day.

Yours, J. Damme

'It would be a good idea, it seems to me, for you to order now a neat defensive jacket for yourself, for there [in London] they make the best and the cheapest ones.'

Margaret Paston's premonitions were all too accurate. On 28 January, as her husband later said in a petition to the king, Lord Moleyns

'sent to the said mansion riotous people to the number of a thousand... arrayed in manner of war with cuirasses, body armour, leather jackets, headpieces, knives, bow, arrows, shields, guns, pans with fire and burning tinder in them, long crowbars for pulling down houses, ladders, pickaxes with which they mined the walls, and long trees with which they broke up gates and doors, and thus came into the said mansion. The wife of your petitioner was in the house, and twelve people with her, whom they drove out of the said mansion, and they mined through the walls of the room where the wife of your petitioner was and carried her out of the gates; and they cut through the posts supporting the house and let them fall. They broke up all the rooms and chests in the said mansion, and rifled them; and as in a robbery they carried off the goods, clothes and money that your petitioner and his servants had there, to the value of £200, and sold part of it, gave part of it away and divided the rest amongst themselves, to the great and outrageous hurt of your petitioner, saying openly that if they had found your petitioner there and one John Damme who is his adviser and various other servants of his, they would have been killed.'

Margaret Paston took refuge with John Damme a mile away at Sustead. She did her best to put her husband's case to the men at Gresham, and a fortnight after her ejection was able to report some degree of apparent success, though some of Moleyns' followers were still very hostile:

15 February, 1449

'I am told that the Lord Moleyns will keep Shrovetide at John Winter's place. His man had a letter last Thursday; what news they had I do not know, but early the next morning Thomas Bampton, one of Lord Moleyns' men, rode off with a letter to his lord, and those who are at Gresham are waiting for an urgent reply to the letter. Barow and Hegon and all Lord Moleyns' men who were at Gresham when you left are still there, except Bampton, and someone else has come in his place; and I gather that they are to stay here until their lord comes. [I wrote] to Barow as you ordered me to ask why they threatened men [. . .] Goneld and other servants and well-wishers of yours were named as having been threatened; [but he] swore openly that they were never threatened. But I know that the opposite is true, because his companions lay in wait several days and nights around Goneld's, Purry's and Bek's places. And some of them went into Bek's and Purry's houses and asked where they were; and they were told that they were out, and they answered that they would meet them some other time. And from various other things I know that if they could have caught them they would either have killed or badly wounded them.

'I sent Katherine with the message I have mentioned, because I could not get any of the men to go, and sent James Halman and Harry Holt with her; and she asked Barow to give her an answer to her message, and also asked whether the men in question could live in peace, saying that otherwise some other remedy would be found. And he made her welcome, and the men who were with her, and said that he would like to speak to me, if it did not displease me. And Katherine said to him that she thought that I would not want to speak to him. And he said that he would come past this place when he was out hunting that afternoon, and no one would come with him except Hegon and one of his own men. And in the afternoon they came and sent a message to me to ask if they could speak to me; they stayed outside the gates, and I came out to them and spoke to them outside, asking them to excuse me for not taking them into the place. I said that because they were not friendly towards the owner of the place, I would not take it on myself to bring them in to meet his lady. They agreed that I acted for the best, and then we walked out and asked them to answer my previous message. They said that they had brought me an answer that they hoped would please me, and told me how they had consulted all their fellows about the matters I had raised before. They were prepared to undertake that none of those who had been named would be hurt, nor any of the men belonging to you, by them or any of their companions; and they assured me of this on their word of honour. Nevertheless, I do not trust their promises, because I find them untrue in other things.

'I gathered from them that they were weary of their doings. Barow swore to me on his word of honour that he would have preferred to lose forty shillings twice over than have been ordered by his lord to come to Gresham, and he said that he was very sorry that it had come about, because he knew you beforehand; he was very sorry for what had been done. I said to him that he ought to be sympathetic to you and others who had been ejected from estates, because he himself had been ejected in the same way. He said that he was, and told me that he had petitioned my lord of Suffolk several times, and would continue to do so until he gets his possessions back again. I said that you had petitioned Lord Moleyns several times about the manor of Gresham, since you were ejected, and could never get a reasonable answer from him, so you had re-entered the manor, since you thought that this was the best thing to do. He said he would never blame my lord of Suffolk for taking over his estates, because he said his lordship was put up to it on information given to him by a false villain. And I said to him that the business between you and Lord Moleyns is the same: I told him that I knew that he did not embark on it because he had any title or right to the manor of Gresham, but only did so on the information of a false villain. I did not name any names, but I think they knew whom I meant. We had much other conversation which would take a long time to write about. I informed them that it had been said that I could not live so close to them as I was for long; and they swore that it was never said, and denied other such things, including much that I know was indeed said.

'I hear it said that you and John Damme are always threatened, and that although you are in London you will be met there just as though you were here, so I beg you with all my heart to beware how you go; and to have a good company with you when you go out. Lord Moleyns has a company of brothel-haunters with him who do not care what they do, and such men are most to be dreaded. Those who are at Gresham say that they have not done as much harm to you as they were ordered to do.

'Robert Laverawns is much better, and I hope he will recover. He says openly that he will make a complaint about his injury, and I think that Bek will do so too, and he has cause for it. Bek and Purry dare not stay at home until they hear different news. I would not like John Damme to come home until the county is in a different state than it is now. I pray that God may grant that it will soon be otherwise. I beg you with all my heart to send word of how you are and how your affairs are going, for on my word of honour I cannot really be at ease in my heart, nor will be until I hear news of how you are.

'Most of your stuff that was at Gresham has been sold and given away. Barow and his companion spoke to me very pleasantly, and it seems to me that would be glad to please me. They said that they would do any service and kindness they could, if it lay in their power to do anything for me, except insofar as it concerned their lord's right.

'I said to them that as far as the "service" they had done for you and me, I would not want them to do it again either to you or me. They said I could have had whatever I asked of them at Gresham, and as much as I would. I said on the contrary, that if I had my way I would neither have left the place nor the goods that were in it. They said that the goods were not worth very much. I said you would not have exchanged the goods that were in the place when they broke in for a hundred pounds. They said that the goods which they saw there were hardly worth £20.

'As for your mother and mine, she is well, blessed be God, and has only good news so far, blessed be God.

'The blessed Trinity have you in their keeping and send you health and good fortune in all your affairs. Written at Sustead on the Saturday after St Valentine's day.

'Here no one dares say a good word for you in the county; may God change that!'

Yours M.P.

A fortnight later, Margaret left Sustead, because of the threats that she 'would not live so close to them [i.e. the mob at Gresham] for long', which implied that she would be kidnapped and forcibly removed. She reported to her husband on developments from the safe haven of Norwich.

28 February, 1449
'*Right worshipful husband*, I commend myself to you, wishing with all my heart to hear that you are well, and begging that you will not be angry at my leaving the place where you left me. On my word, such news was brought to me by various people who are sympathetic to you and me that I did not dare stay there any longer. I will tell you who the people were when you come home. They let me know that various of Lord Moleyns' men said that if they could get their hands on me they would carry me off and keep me in the castle. They wanted you to get me out again, and said that it would not cause you much heart-ache. After I heard this news, I could not rest easy until I was here, and I did not dare go out of the place where I was until I was ready to ride away. Nobody in the place knew that I was leaving except the lady of the house, until an hour before I went. And I told her that I would come here to have clothes made for myself and the children, which I wanted made, and said I thought I would be here a

39

fortnight or three weeks. Please keep the reason for my departure a secret until I talk to you, for those who warned me do not on any account want it known.

'I spoke to your mother as I came this way, and she offered to let me stay in this town, if you agree. She would very much like us to stay at her place, and will send me such things as she can spare so that I can set up house until you can get a place and things of your own to set up a household. Please let me know by the man who brings this what you would like me to do. I would be very unhappy to live so close to Gresham as I was until this matter is completely settled between you and Lord Moleyns.

'Barow told me that there was no better evidence in England than that Lord Moleyns has for [his title to] the manor of Gresham. I told him that I supposed the evidence was of the kind that William Hasard said yours was, and that the seals were not yet cold. That, I said, was what I expected his lord's evidence to be like. I said I knew that your evidence was such that no one could have better evidence, and the seals on it were two hundred years older than he was. Then Barow said to me that if he came to London while you were there he would have a drink with you, to quell any anger there was between you. He said that he only acted as a servant, and as he was ordered to do. Purry will tell you about the conversation between Barow and me when I came from Walsingham. I beg you with all my heart, for reverence of God, beware of Lord Moleyns and his men, however pleasantly they speak to you, and do not eat or drink with them; for they are so false that they cannot be trusted. And please take care when you eat or drink in any other men's company, for no one can be trusted.

'I beg you with all my heart that you will be kind enough to send me word how you are, and how your affairs are going, by the man who brings this. I am very surprised that you do not send me more news than you have done.

'Roger Foke of Sparham sent a message to me saying that he dare not go out of his house because of the case Heydon and Wymondham have brought against him, because he has been threatened with being taken to prison if he can be caught. Heydon sent Spendlove and some others to wait where he was, and to arrest him and take him to

Norwich Castle, and Roger is so afraid that his fear is making him ill, and unless he gets help soon it will be the death of him. So please provide a remedy for him so that he can move around freely, because it is bad both for him and for your livestock. Your enclosures and pastures are all lying open because he cannot go out to mend the fences, and your sheep are not looked after as they should be, because there is no shepherd apart from Hodge's son; no other shepherd dares to stay on the common because the Witchingham men threaten to beat them if they come on their common. And unless your beasts can graze there it will do them much harm, unless you get more pasture than that which they already have apart from the common. . .

'The parson of Sparham's daughter and others have been boasting and saying that you have been shot at once, and unless you are careful you will get more before Easter. You will lose Sporle and Swainsthorpe as well unless you behave well, before the Gresham business is finished. I am told that, as for Gresham, Lord Moleyns will not claim it by entail or by evidence, but by enfeoffment of one of his ancestors who died in possession of it; and Swainsthorpe is to be claimed in the same way. How Sporle is to be claimed I do not know; but if any such move is afoot I am warning you so that you are aware of it. Thomas Skepping said, when he came from London, to a man who he thought would not have repeated it, that you are likely to lose the manor of Sporle within a very short time. As for the plaints in the hundred court, Purry will tell you what is done, and about other things as well.

'The Holy Trinity have you in his keeping. Written at Norwich on the Friday after Ash Wednesday.'

Sporle, an isolated holding of the Pastons near Swaffham, would have been difficult for the Pastons to defend; Swainsthorpe, five miles south of Norwich, was at least nearer their main centre of power. This was also the time when an attack on Oxnead by John Hauteyn's supporters seemed likely, and in the midst of all this Edmund Paston died, just when the family's enemies seemed to be getting the upper hand. At the end of March, Lord Moleyns wrote to the tenants at Gresham assuring them that 'the title of right that I have to the lordship of

Gresham shall be known in a short time, and will be established at law, so that all of you who have favoured my cause will be glad of it.' Moleyns also wrote to his other cronies in the county to drum up support, as Margaret Paston soon reported to her husband:

2 April, 1449

'*Right worshipful husband*, I commend myself to you. This is to let you know that my cousin Clere dined with me today, and she told me that Heydon was with her late yesterday evening. And he told her that he had a letter from Lord Moleyns, and showed the same letter to her, asking him to tell his friends and well-wishers in this county that he thanks them for their goodwill and for what they have done for him; and he asked Heydon to say to Richard Ernold of Cromer that he was sorry and had been badly served when his men attacked him, for he said that he did not want his men to attack anyone in the county without very good cause; and as for what was done to you, if it could be proved that he had done anything other than was right as far as your moveable goods were concerned, he would compensate you for it so that you would have reason to be grateful. And he asked Heydon to let it be known in the county that he would do so, if he had done otherwise than he should have done... The Lord Moleyns also wrote in this letter to say that he would firmly support those that had been his friends in the Gresham affair, with his body and his goods, and asked Heydon to tell them not to be in the least afraid, for what had been done should stay as it was.

'My mother-in-law asks you to send my brother William at Cambridge a nominal and a book of sophistry [grammar books] of my brother Edmund's, which he asked my mother-in-law to send to William the last time he spoke to her.

'The blissful Trinity have you in his keeping. Written at Norwich in haste on the Wednesday before Palm Sunday.'

Yours, M.P.

John Paston, for his part, was doing what he could to find support in London; what he chiefly needed was a patron with influence in the courts, and his first choice seems to have been Thomas Daniel, the castellan of Castle Rising, who was one of Henry VI's close advisers and a member of the royal household since at least 1444. He was perhaps an unwise choice, since he seems to have sat on the fence politically, and by 1449 he was regarded as a supporter of Suffolk. The question of patronage was of course complex and differences between supporters of the same nobleman by no means uncommon. Margaret, trying to rally his supporters in Norfolk, was dubious about the effectiveness of Daniel, and told her husband of her doubts:

'*Right worshipful husband*, I commend myself to you, and desire with all my heart to hear how you are. I have been to Swainsthorpe and have spoken to Kokett, and he says that he will do as you told me to tell him to do. And I have spoken to the sexton, and said to him what you told me to say, and he asked me like a faithful servant how your affairs were going. I told him that you had been promised favours, and I hoped that things would go well; and he said that he thought that D. would act on your behalf, but that he was never a quick worker. He said that he knew a man who used his influence for him over some business, and he kept promising that he would get it settled in his favour, but as long as he asked him to look after it, he could never get the business brought to a good conclusion. When he thought that he would get nowhere by his request, he talked to Fines, who is now speaker of the parliament, and asked him to act for him in the matter, and gave him a reward, and very soon afterwards the affair was settled.

'And the said sexton and other people that wish you well in this affair, have advised me to advise you to find some other means of going about it and to find other people who will press your business harder than those who you have spoken to about it up to now. Various people have said to me that they are sure that unless you have the duke of Suffolk's favour while the world is as it is, you can never live in peace. So I beg you with all my heart that you will do what you can to get his favour and love to ease all the affairs you have to deal with, and to ease my heart as well. Otherwise, on my word, I shall be frightened of the outcome of both the affairs you have in hand now, and of others that have not come up yet, unless he will act for you and favour you.

'I beg you with all my heart to send me word how you are and how your business is going; and please let me have the things of which

James has a list as quickly as you can, and please buy me a piece of black buckram for me to line a gown with. I want to buy a purple gown for the summer and to let into the collar the satin you gave me as a hood, and I cannot get any good buckram in this town to line it with.

'The Holy Trinity have you in his keeping and send you health and good fortune in all your affairs. Written at Norwich the Friday after Crouchmass day.'

Yours, M.P.

John Paston was also involved in negotiations over a possible marriage between Stephen Scrope, the fifty-year-old stepson of Sir John Fastolf, and his sister Elizabeth. Fastolf, a soldier who had made his name in the wars against France, was a near neighbour of Margaret Paston's parents: his newly-built fortress at Caister was within sight of her old home at Mautby. Elizabeth Paston was anxious for the match, because her life at home was far from pleasant; she and her mother were at loggerheads, and the result was reported to John Paston on June 29 by Elizabeth Clere, a neighbour of his mother's in whom his sister had confided. After discussing the merits of a match with Scrope, she continues:

'If you can get a better match, I would advise you to do so in as short a time as you decently can, because she was never in such sorrow as she is nowadays. She is not allowed to speak to anyone, whoever comes, and she is unable to speak to my man or to her mother's servants, unless she manages to deceive her mother. Since Easter she has usually been beaten once or twice a day, and sometimes thrice a day, and her head has been cut in two or three places.

'So she sent a message to me by Friar Newton in great secrecy, and begged me to send you a letter about her trouble, and to ask you to be a good brother to her, because she trusts you. She says that if his papers show that his children and hers will inherit and she will get a reasonable settlement, she has heard so much of his birth and estate that, if you agree she will take him, whether her mother wants her to or not; even though she is told that he is a plain man, because she says that men will regard her more highly if she behaves as she should towards him.

'Cousin, I am told that there is a handsome man in your Inn whose father died recently, and if you think he would be a better match than Scrope, you ought to try to arrange it, and give Scrope a pleasant reply, so that he is not rejected until you are sure of getting someone better. He said when he was with me that unless he gets a favourable answer from you, he will not go further in the matter, because he is not allowed to see my cousin your sister. He says that he should have seen her, even if she was of greater rank than she is, and that makes him think that your mother is not well disposed towards the match; and I have sent word to my cousin your mother of this. So, cousin, please think of this business, for sorrow often causes women to behave otherwise than they should, and I know you would be sorry if that happened to her.

'Cousin, please burn this letter, so that none of your men or anyone else sees it, for if my cousin your mother knew that I had sent you this letter, she would never love me for it.

'I will write no more for the moment, but the Holy Ghost have you in his keeping. Written in haste on St Peter's day by candlelight.'

From your cousin Elizabeth Clere

The match came to nothing, and Elizabeth had to endure another five years or more of life at Oxnead before she was sent to board in Lady Pole's household in London. A year or so later she did at last marry; at least two other matches had been proposed for her since 1450.

Gresham, however, remained Margaret Paston's main concern. Early in the following year the matter was still unresolved, and greater political events were beginning to overshadow local disorders, as the news that she had for her husband on 12 March 1450 shows:

'*Right worshipful husband*, I commend myself to you, and desire with all my heart to hear that you are well. Thank you for the letter that you sent me. . .

'I have spoken to John Damme to get him to do as you sent word in your letter, and he says that he will gladly do as you wish. James Gloys was over there since he came from London, and spoke to Henry Goneld. Henry told them that he had heard that Partridge had sent a letter to the lime-burner telling him to cut the rushes at Gresham; and they have been cut and carried to Marriott's place at Beckham. Henry says that they say in Gresham that Partridge sent word to his home that he would not be coming home until he came with his lord; that, he said, would be in a short time, and he would lodge at John Winter's place. As for Capron, he is still living at Gresham, and he and the others who are against you say that even if you enter the manor again you will never hold it for long in peace.

'William Butt, who is with Sir John Heveningham, came home from London yesterday; and he said plainly to his master and to many other people that the duke of Suffolk is pardoned and has his men waiting on him again, and is very well at ease and merry; and is in the king's favour and respected by all the lords as much as he ever was.

'There are many ships off Yarmouth and Cromer, who have done much harm and taken many Englishmen and put them in great distress and ransomed them for great sums. These enemies are so bold that they come ashore and play on Caister Sands and other places, so much at home as if they were Englishmen. People are very much afraid that they will do much harm this summer unless great preparations are made to resist them. I have no other news at the moment.

'The blissful Trinity have you in his keeping. Written at Norwich on St Gregory's day.'

Yours, M.P.

In fact the news from London was untrue; but in days when there were few official sources of news, hearsay and travellers' tales played a great part: though to be fair to Margaret, she only reports the story of Suffolk's return to favour as hearsay, perhaps hoping that this unwelcome report was unfounded, as indeed it was. The news of his death was reported to John Paston not only by William Lomnor (p 29 above) but also on the following day by John Crane, who added that there was much activity with petitions now that Suffolk's influence was removed, and advised John to get his in quickly: Suffolk had many other adversaries and victims. A week later Thomas Denys, a servant of the earl of Oxford, wrote to say that Paston's patron Daniel had been made steward of the duchy of Lancaster and that his enemy

Sir Thomas Tuddenham was likely to lose his place. Denys had his own reasons for writing as well, since he ended his letter;

'Please think about my request to my mistress your wife about mistress Anne, for in good faith I have completely won over my lady since you went, so that I have her promise that she will favour me and help me, by the faith of her body.'

We shall see the outcome of Denys' wooing of Anne or Agnes, a friend of the Pastons, later. His political news was important, as the longed-for relief from the attacks of Heydon and Tuddenham seemed to be at hand. Although Lord Moleyns endeavoured to take out writs secretly against John and his followers over the Gresham affair in July, William Lomnor saw the papers and foiled this attempt. On the other hand, James Gresham was unable to get Lord Moleyns to agree to hand over Gresham to a third party, even though the new lord chancellor was apparently favourably inclined to John Paston's case.

But national events now overshadowed any personal lawsuits. On June 29, the bishop of Salisbury, an old friend of Suffolk, was dragged from the church at Edington in Wiltshire and murdered; that same day, a rebellious mob from Kent led by a certain Jack Cade marched to Blackheath, the scene of Wat Tyler's revolt nearly seventy years before, to threaten London. The king retreated to Kenilworth, and on July 2 the rebels seized the City.

The next day two unpopular nobles, Lord Say and his son-in-law Crowmer, sheriff of Kent, were beheaded, and some pillaging took place. On July 5, the mayor attempted to prevent Cade from re-entering the City, and after fierce fighting which lasted all night, succeeded in doing so. Negotiations were opened and a general pardon was accepted by the rebels, who retired home, with the exception of Cade; he knew that such a pardon was no safeguard for a ringleader, and he had earlier misdeeds to account for. He released the prisoners in two London gaols, and made off with them into Kent, but was mortally wounded and captured a week later. Fifteen years later, John Payn, one of Sir John Fastolf's servants, described the rebellion in a petition to John Paston as Fastolf's executor. Fastolf was unpopular because he was held responsible for recent disasters in France, disasters

47

which were continuing: on 19 August James Gresham was to write
to John Paston: 'Cherbourg is gone, and now we have not a foot of
land in Normandy; men fear that Calais will soon be besieged.'
Fastolf had sent Payn to investigate as soon as he heard that the rebels
were approaching, and Payn describes what happened next:

'My master Sir John Fastolf . . . commanded your petitioner to take a
man and two of the best horses that were in his stable to ride to the
common people of Kent and to get a list of the reasons why they had
come. And so I did, and as soon as I came to Blackheath the captain
[i.e. Jack Cade] made the rebels take me; and in order to save my
master's horses, I made my companion ride off with both of them.
And I was brought immediately before the captain of Kent, and the
captain demanded of me what the reason for my coming there was and
why I had made my companion slink off with the horses. I said that I
had come to greet my wife's brothers and other friends and relations
of mine who were there. And there was a man there who said to the
captain that I was one of Sir John Fastolf's men, and the two horses
were Sir John Fastolf's; and then the captain raised a cry of treason
against me throughout the camp, and took me to four parts of the
field with one of the duke of Exeter's heralds in front of me in the
duke's coat of arms, who made four *Oyez* at the four parts of the field.
He proclaimed through the herald that I was sent there to spy, and to
find out how powerful they were and what their equipment was like,
by the greatest traitor in England and France (so the captain proclaimed
at the time) one Sir John Fastolf, knight, who had reduced all the
garrisons in Normandy, Le Mans and Maine and had caused the king
to lose his title and right of inheritance overseas. And besides, he said,
the said Sir John Fastolf had garrisoned his place with veterans from
Normandy and war supplies in order to destroy the common people
of Kent when they came to Southwark, and for that, he said plainly,
I should lose my head. And so I was taken at once and led to the captain's tent, and an axe and a block were brought out, for my execution:
and then Master Poynings, your brother-in-law, and other friends of
mine came and stopped the captain, and said a hundred or two would
die if I died, and so my life was saved for the moment.

'Then I was made to swear to the captain and the common people that I would go to Southwark and equip myself as best I could and return to help them; that cost me more than 27s that day, given to the common people. So I came to my Master Fastolf and brought him the list of their grievances, and told him everything, advising to put away his weapons and dismiss his soldiers. He did so, and he and all his household went to the tower, except for Bettes and one Matthew Brain. If I had not been with them, the common people would have burnt his place and all those of his tenants. This cost me, out of my own pocket, more than £4 in meat and drink. And despite this the captain had me seized at the White Hart at Southwark, and commanded Lovelase to strip me of my equipment, which he did. He took a fine gown of grey woollen cloth, furred with fine beaver, and a pair of brigandines [body armour] covered with blue velvet and gilt nails, with leg-armour; the value of the gown and the brigandines was £8.

'And the captain sent some of his followers to my room in your houses, and there they broke open my chest and took away a bond of mine for £36 due to me from a priest at St Paul's, and another bond due from a knight for £10, and my purse with five gold rings, and 16s 8d in gold and silver, a complete suit of Milan armour, and a gown of fine grey-blue furred with martens, and two gowns, one furred with sheepskin and the other lined with frieze-cloth; and they wanted to cut off my head when they had stripped me at the White Hart. And my Master Poynings and my friends saved me, and I was shut up until the night of the battle at London Bridge, and then, at night, the captain put me into the battle on the bridge, and I was wounded and hurt, almost mortally; I was in the battle for six hours and could not get out of it. And four times before then I was carried around through Kent and Sussex, and they wanted to cut off my head.

'And in Kent, where my wife lived, they took away all our moveable goods and wanted to hang my wife and five of my children, and left her nothing except her kirtle and smock. And soon after that riot, Bishop Ross impeached me before the queen; and so I was arrested by the queen's order and put in the Marshalsea prison. There I was in very great hardship and fear of my life, and was threatened with hanging, drawing and quartering, because they wanted to make me impeach my master Fastolf for treason, and because I refused, they took me to Westminster and wanted to send me to the coal-house at Windsor; but a cousin of my wife and a cousin of mine who were both yeomen of the crown went to the king and obtained grace and a charter of pardon.'

Par le vostre, Payn J.

Cade's rebellion, though quickly over, was a symptom of general unrest. In August, the duke of York returned to England from semi-exile as governor of Ireland; and on him the hopes of those who wanted changes in the government were centred. A new parliament met in November, and there was much political manoeuvring, both over the elections and – of more concern to the Pastons – over attempts to get a commission of *oyer et terminer* for Norfolk and Suffolk, a special court designed to deal with grievances or problems of a troubled region or to settle difficult cases. This was directed against the activities of Sir Thomas Tuddenham and John Heydon, and was first rumoured at the beginning of August. But Moleyns, with whom John Paston was naturally most concerned, had managed to get a writ from the king requiring Paston to respite any attempt against him, or against any other of his servants, supporters or tenants because of him, until such time as he could appear personally. The mood of the times is reflected in a letter to John Paston from Justice Yelverton's clerk, reporting on affairs in London: no one was sure who really held power, and whether the old order had really given way to a new and better state of affairs. Sir William Oldhall was to be the speaker of commons a month later.

6 October, 1450

'*Sir*, may it please you, I was in my lord of York's house and I heard many more things than those about which my master has written to you. I heard many things in Fleet Street. But, sir, my lord [of York] was with the king, and he put such a front on matters that all the king's household were and are very frightened: and my lord has presented a petition to the king and asked for many things, which are much after the commons' heart. They all want justice and to put those who are indicted under arrest, without sureties or mainprise, to be tried by law

as the law will have it; insomuch that on Monday Sir W. Oldhall was
with the king at Westminster for more than two hours, and was well
received by the king. The king asked Sir W. Oldhall to speak to his
cousin York and ask him to favour John Penycook, and to write to his
tenants to allow Penycook to go and collect his rents and revenues in
the duke's lordships. And Sir William Oldhall replied to the king,
asking him to excuse his lord, for even if my lord wrote under his seal
bearing his arms, his tenants would not obey. In the same way, when
Sir Thomas Hoo met my lord of York beyond St Albans, the West
Country men fell on him and would have killed him, if Sir William
Oldhall had not been there; and for that the West Country men
wanted to attack Sir William and kill him, or so he told the king.

'Sir, Borle, Yonge and Josse are doing their best for Heydon and
Tuddenham with Sir William Oldhall, and are offering more than
two thousand pounds to have his favour, and so the only remedy is to
warn the Swaffham men to meet my lord [of York] next Friday, coming to Pickenham on horseback as well turned out as possible, and to
give some petition to my lord about Sir Thomas Tuddenham, Heydon
and Prentice, and to complain about them and call them extortioners,
and beg my lord to carry out swift sentence on them. And my master
advises you to persuade the mayor and all the aldermen [of Norwich]
to ride to my lord, and get petitions drawn up and given to my lord;
and get the whole town to decry Heydon, Tuddenham, Wymondham and Prentys and all their false supporters, telling my lord how
much damage they have done to the city. Get it done with as much
lamenting as you can; for, sir, unless my lord hear some foul tale
about them and some hideous noise and crying, by my faith they are
otherwise likely to come into favour. And therefore, sir, remember
this business.

'Sir, I also spoke with William Norwich and asked after Lord
Moleyns and how he stood with my lord; and he told me that he was
very much out of favour and that my lord of York does not love him.
William Norwich told me that he could undertake to bring you to my
lord and make him your patron; and, sir, my master advised you that
you should not hesitate, but should get his patronage.

'Sir, beware of Heydon, for he wants to destroy you, by my

faith. The Lord Scales and Sir William Oldhall have been reconciled.

'Sir, canvass to be elected knight of the shire [i.e. MP] and speak to my master, Stapleton, to get him to do so as well. Sir, the whole of Swaffham, if they are told, will vote for you. Sir, speak to Thomas Denys and take his good advice about it. Sir, speak to Denys and tell him to remove his garrison at Reydon, for there is no other way out except death for Daniel and those who have been indicted. Sir, canvass the mayor to get John Damme [recorder of Norwich] or William Jenney as burgess [MP] for the city of Norwich. Tell him that he can be an MP, just as Yonge is at Bristol, or the recorder is for London, and just as the recorder of Coventry is for the city of Coventry, and so on in many places in England. Also, sir, think of Yarmouth, and arrange that John Jenney or Lomnor or some good man is burgess for Yarmouth. Arrange that the Jenneys shall be in parliament, for they are good speakers.

'Sir, it would be wise for my lord of Oxford to wait on my lord of York. In good faith, sir, think on all these affairs. I have much more that I could have written if I could remember, but I have had no time, by my faith. Please excuse my poor rough writing.

'John Damme should beware of Lord Moleyns, and the city too, for he will commit a felony if he can get at his men. And sir, if he comes to Norwich, make sure that a good company is ready to attend the mayor, for it is said here that they are no better than beasts.

'Sir, my mother told me to write to you to persuade the mayor and all the aldermen to beseech my lord for justice on the men who are indicted, and to beg my lord to speak to the king about it. And sir, in the different parts of the town where my lord comes, there should be organised groups of the common people to cry out to my lord for justice on the men who are indicted, and name their names, especially Tuddenham, Heydon, Wymondham and Prentys.

'Sir, I send you a copy of the petition that my lord of York presented to the king, have copies circulated in the city, for the love of God; may he have you in his keeping.

'Written on St Faith's day in haste.'

By your servant W. Wayte

Yelverton himself wrote anonymously to John Paston about the same time, warning him that Lord Moleyns had some plot afoot to bring his rabble into Norfolk and that Tuddenham and Heydon were going to try to bribe their way into getting control of the Norfolk elections: 'they will spend £2000 to get in there, and that would be a pity. Spend something of your own now, and get influence and friends, "for on that hangs all the law and the prophets".' The following month Yelverton wrote to Sir John Fastolf:

'*My most worshipful and most trusted master*, I commend myself to you, thanking you for the many great and gentle kindnesses you have done me, and for the great assistance from your man, and your horses as well.

'As for news from this part of the world, people here are in a strange mood, and many of them are hostile to Sir Thomas Tuddenham and Heydon. If they are encouraged by election of a good sheriff and under-sheriff, they may get a remedy by due process of law; otherwise great inconvenience is likely to follow. Therefore, sir, for the good of the whole country, approach the king, my lord chancellor and all the other lords as you think is best for the business in question.

'Also, sir, if anyone complains against me, through Lord Scales or anyone else's doing, or through a petition presented by Brygg or any other man put up to it by them, please speak up for me to save my reputation, which I know they can only hurt by wrongful accusations. Speak to the king, my lord chancellor, my lord of Winchester, my Lord Cromwell, and in other quarters as seems fit, so that no credit is given to stories against me in my absence.

'Also, sir, see that William Jenney and Brain, the clerk of the sessions, are sent here as quickly as possible. And, sir, my cousin Paston and my brother Clere can tell you much more, which I would write to you about if I had time; but I will soon send you more news from this part of the world, by the grace of God. May he have you in his holy keeping.'

By your old servant, William Yelverton, Justice

Although the commission of *oyer et terminer* began work at the end of 1450, Wayte was still writing to John Paston early in 1451 to arrange more demonstrations against Tuddenham and Heydon. But elsewhere the death of the duke of Suffolk had begun to make some difference. Moleyns' men at Gresham seem to have withdrawn, and John Paston was able to reclaim the manor peaceably at some time in January or February. Although Moleyns threatened to come and eject him again, this was the end of the matter. But elsewhere things were not going so well, as Margaret Paston reported:

'*Right worshipful husband,* I commend myself to you, and wish with all my heart to hear that you are well. This is to let you know that Henry Halman's wife sent word to me last Saturday that Prentys is threatening her husband, and John Robyns as well, for things that Prentys says they have done to him. He says he will make them so busy before he has finished with them that he will make them not worth a penny, and they are afraid that he will get them bound over if he has the power to do so.

'It is said here that the king is to come to this part of the world and Sir Thomas Tuddenham and Heydon are in his favour; and it is also said that they will have as much influence hereabouts as they ever had. Many more people are sorry about this than are glad. Sir Thomas Tuddenham's men and Heydon's are spreading the rumour everywhere that their masters will come home prosperous and be as comfortable as they ever were.

'As for your request that I should enquire where any goods of yours are, I do not know what to do about it; because if one man were seen with some of your goods, and we had it off him, others who have more of them would beware, and put away any goods of yours that they have. I think that John Osbern will tell you a good way of finding out where much of it is when you come home.

'James Gloys is back at Gresham, and I think John Damme will tell what he has done there. Your tenants would be glad if some of your men could live with them, because they are in great confusion as to what to do; the other party speak so threateningly that it makes the tenants very afraid that you will not enjoy peace for long. I am sending you a letter from Francis Costard by Colin, saying what he wants done. I was also told that Lord Moleyns was likely to have a case against you at Thetford at the next assize. A man who is friendly towards you told me that he had been told so, and warned me in secret. It is as well to beware of their tricks.

'Please send me word quickly if you want your livery to be red, as you thought, or not. Please also bring two good hats for your sons, because I cannot get any in this town.

'This is all the news I can send you at the moment.

'The Holy Trinity have you in his keeping. Written at Norwich on the first Monday of Lent.'

Yours, M.P.

The work of the *oyer et terminer* commission proceeded slowly, and early in May came to a disastrous end as far as the Pastons were concerned. Despite Yelverton's support, the other judges were hostile, and one, Prisot, openly took Tuddenham and Heydon's side. Thomas Howes, a member of Sir John Fastolf's household, wrote to his master on May 9 describing what happened:

'. . . when the counsel for the city of Norwich, for the town of Swaffham, for you, for my Master Inglose, for Paston and for many other plaintiffs had asserted and declared both in writing and in their speeches before the judges, the offences at law, the judges, by their wilfulness, could not find it in their heart to pay the least attention, not even a nod or a wink, but scorned it. God reform such partiality! Because Prisot knew that if the sessions of the *oyer et terminer* were held at Norwich, where they began, they would not go as Tuddenham, Heydon and their cronies wanted, as it might do elsewhere, he adjourned them to Walsingham, where they have most influence, to be held there on Tuesday, May 4.

'Knowing this, my master of Yelverton, Jenney and others had a good idea how the *oyer et terminer* would be carried out, for it was the most favourable place for them in the whole county, and all their friends, knights and squires and gentlemen who would do exactly as they wanted were summoned there. And the said Tuddenham, Heydon and other oppressors of their set came down there with, so I understand, 400 or more horsemen. Considering how their supporters had gathered there at their request, it was very dangerous and frightening for any of the plaintiffs to appear; and not one of the plaintiffs or complainants was there, except for your trusty and faithful supporter John Paston.'

Yelverton was clearly outnumbered, and could do no more than control Prisot's outbursts; and John Jermyn, the new sheriff of Norfolk, was less favourable than had been hoped. John Paston had been warned of the situation by friends on May 2, who wrote from Walsingham that

'the sheriff is not wholly on our side as he was, for now he wants to show us only part of his friendship. And also there is a great crowd of people here, and few friends as far as we can tell at the moment. So think seriously whether it would be best to come yourself or to send someone, for we will do our best to prevail on your behalf.'

The assizes ended without any sentence against Tuddenham and Heydon, and John Paston's case against Lord Moleyns, which he seems to have managed to bring despite the king's letter in September, was also dismissed. However, John had achieved his main object, the re-taking of Gresham, and the power of his opponents, though by no means totally destroyed, had undoubtedly diminished. Margaret's letters to him in the summer of 1451, while they mention some disturbances in the county, are much more concerned with domestic detail, such as that of June 3 about the possible purchase of a new house in St Laurence's parish of Norwich, and requests for 'white ointment' and to 'remember your pretty daughter's girdle'. On July 1, she had little more than local gossip to report:

'I went to dinner at Toppys on St Peter's day. There my Lady Felbrigg and the other ladies would have liked to have had you there; they said that they would all have been more cheerful if you had been there. My cousin Toppys is very worried and wants to hear good news of her brother's business. She told me that an appointment had been made for next Monday between her brother and Sir Andrew Hugard and Wyndham. Please let me know what happens, and how your own affairs are going.

'Please also send me a pot of treacle very soon, for both I and your daughter have not been at all well, since you left here. And one of the tallest young men of this parish is ill, and has very bad catarrh; what will become of him, God knows. My aunt asks to be remembered to you, and asks you to do the things listed on the note which I am sending in with this letter, as you think best.

'Sir Harry Inglose has passed to God tonight, on whose soul God have mercy, and was carried to St Faith's at nine o'clock today, where he is to be buried. If you want to buy any of his things, please let me know quickly and I will speak to Robert Inglose and to Witchingham about it. I think they are the executors.'

In a postscript she adds: 'Don't trust the sheriff, however friendly his language.'

Five days later, she reminds John that he has not yet bought the girdle as requested on June 3, and asks for 'another sugarloaf because my old one is finished'. This time the postcript excuses the fact that she is writing on a sheet of paper which has a piece cut out of it: 'Paper is scarce.'

Meanwhile at Paston, John's mother was still involved in the old dispute over the moving of the road; she was evidently trying to build a wall to enclose either the farmyard or perhaps a garden of some kind. The villagers were angry about this, though it is hard to gather any reason: but as soon as work started there was trouble:

'On Thursday the wall was built up to a yard high; and a good while before entering it rained so hard that they wanted to cover the wall and stop work. So much rain had fallen that the water stands a foot deep on the Balls' side. And on Friday after the consecration of the host someone came from the direction of the church and took down everything that was on it and trod on the wall and broke some of it and went across. I cannot find out who it was. And Warren King's wife, as she went over the stile, cursed Ball and said that he had given away the road, and John Paston's words proved it; and afterwards King's people and others came and shouted at Agnes Ball, saying the same to her. Yesterday evening when I was going to bed the vicar said that Warren King and Warren Harman, between mass and matins, took Robert into the vestry and told him to tell me that the wall should be taken down again.'

Once the wall was built there was further trouble: On November 8, Agnes wrote to John in London.

'... Warren Harman, on the Sunday after Hallowmas, after evensong, said openly in the churchyard that he knew that if the wall was pulled down, even if he was a hundred miles from Paston, I would say that he did it, and he would be blamed. He said, "I don't care who repeats it; even if it costs me twenty nobles, it shall be pulled down again." And Warren's wife said in a loud voice: "All the devils in hell drag her soul to hell for the road she has made!"

'And that evening a certain man came to supper and told me that the patent granted the enclosure of a perch's breadth, and that I had enclosed more than was granted by the patent, so men say. And John Marchall told me that a poor woman came past the watering-place and found the way was blocked, and asked him who had blocked the way; and he said it was done by people who had the power to give, the right to do it, and asked her what could be freer than a gift. And she said she had seen the day when Paston men would not have allowed it.

'And God be with you. Written at Paston on Monday after Hallowmas day.'

By your mother Agnes Paston

A fortnight later there were still mutterings:

'... on the Sunday after evensong Agnes Ball came and saw me in my closet and said good evening, and Clement Spicer was with her. And I asked him what he wanted, and he asked me why I had blocked the king's highway. And I said that I had blocked no highway except my own, and asked him why he had sold my land to John Ball. He swore he had never made an agreement with your father. And I said that if his father had done what he did, he would have been ashamed to say what he said.

'And all the time Warren Harman leaned over the partition and listened to what we said; and he said that the change was a change for the worse, for the town was harmed by it and was a hundred pounds worse off; and I told him that it was rude of him to interfere in business unless he was asked to advise. And he went out boldly with me into the church, and said that blocking the way had cost me twenty nobles, and it would come down again all the same. Also he said that I did well to put men to work to collect money while I was here, but in the end I would lose my expenses. Then he asked me why I had taken away his hay at Walsham, saying that he wished he had known when it was carried away, and he would have prevented it; and I told him it was my own ground, and I would keep it as my own. And he told me to take four acres and go no further; and soon after he left me in the churchyard.'

The following year, there were still protests; on St Mark's day 1452 the men of Paston refused to go in procession further than the church-yard because the traditional procession route had been blocked. The villagers still hoped that the wall would be pulled down, and Agnes Paston was fined in the manor court for blocking the highway. This fine was not paid until 1461, but there is no further mention of the dis-pute; perhaps the conservative villagers eventually came to accept the innovation.

John Paston's affairs in 1452 were much concerned with the entourage of the duke of Norfolk. His dubious ally of earlier years, Thomas Daniel, was back in favour, with the duke's help, and Paston himself attended the duke at Framlingham in March. But the next month, at Norwich, he was attacked by one of the duke's men, as he reported in a letter probably sent to John Clopton, the sheriff of Norfolk.

'*Reverend and right worshipful sir and my good master*, I commend my-self to you. This is to inform you that Charles Nowell and others here committed many riots and assaults in this part of the world; among others, he and five of his fellows set upon me and two of my servants at the cathedral in Norwich; he hit out at me while one of his companions held my arms behind my back; the bearer of this letter will tell you more fully about it. This seemed strange to me, because I believed that I had been his lord's man and had done homage to my lord before Charles knew his lordship, and that my lord was favour-ably disposed to me. I had been with my lord a week before Lent, and he was then so well-disposed to me that I shall always do my best to serve him faithfully. I thought also that I had never given cause to any of my lord's household to wish me harm; and there was no one in that household for whom I would not do whatever I could wish anyone to do for me; and I still would, except for my attacker.'

John goes on to say that he would have brought this to the sheriff's notice before, but he had expected the duke of Norfolk to arrive at Framlingham at any time, and had hoped to settle the affair within the duke's household. But the duke was deep in greater matters. Although he had been a supporter of the duke of York in 1450–1, and was opposed to the court party, now led by Somerset in place of Suffolk, he did not take part in York's armed rising in January 1452, when the latter attempted to seize Henry. Yet he was sufficiently implicated to take the precaution of getting a pardon in June for any part he might have had in York's actions, and clearly felt it inadvisable to leave the court until his position was secure. However, he was eager to strengthen his hand in the country, as Agnes Paston's news on November 16 shows:

'[John Damme] told me that he heard it said that Sir John Fastolf has sold Hellesdon to Boleyn of London, and if that is so, it seems he will sell more besides; so please, if you want my love and blessing, help me and do your duty by seeing that something is bought for your two brothers. I think that Sir John Fastolf, if you spoke to him, would prefer to let his kinsmen have something, rather than strangers. Try him, in my name, about the places to which you think the title is most clear. It is said hereabouts that my lord of Norfolk is saying that Sir John Fastolf has given him Caister, and he wants to have all of it.'

If John's two younger brothers needed lands, his sister needed a husband, as Margaret remarked early in 1453:

'*Right worshipful husband*, I commend myself to you. This is to let you know that I spoke yesterday to your sister, and she told me that she was sorry she could not speak with you before you went. She asks, if you agree, that you should speak to the gentleman in question and imply that you would be well-disposed to the business about which you know. She told me that he has said before that he thought you were not much concerned about it. So she asks you to be a good brother, and try to get a full answer now, either yes or no. For her mother has said to her since you rode off that she is not in favour of it, and it will all come to nothing, and that there is much art in being insincere. She uses such language to her that she thinks it very strange and is very tired of it. So she would rather the matter were settled. She says that she trusts you completely, and will agree to whatever you arrange.

'Master Brackley was here yesterday to speak to you. I talked to him, but he would not tell me what his business was. It is said here that the sessions are to be at Thetford next Saturday, and my lord of Norfolk and others will be there with a great following. We have no other news at the moment.

'The blissful Trinity have you in his keeping. Written at Norwich the Tuesday before Candlemas.

'Please be kind and remember to get me some kind of necklace, and to have my girdle made.

Yours, M.P.

'My cousin Crane commends herself to you, and asks you to remember her affairs, because she cannot sleep at night because of him.'

Marriages were very much in the air. Not only John Paston, but even the queen and the earl of Oxford were involved in matchmaking for acquaintances of the Pastons. On April 17, Queen Margaret came to Norwich. Margaret wrote three days later:

'As for news, the queen came into the town last Tuesday afternoon, and stayed until 3 o'clock on Thursday afternoon. She sent Sharynborn to summon my cousin Elizabeth Clere to her. She did not dare disobey her command, and came to her. When she entered the queen's presence, the queen made much of her, and asked her to take a husband, which I will tell you about afterwards; but all the same, he is no nearer to getting her than before. The queen was very pleased with her reply, and speaks of her very highly, saying that since she came to Norfolk she has seen no lady whom she likes better than her.

'... Please spend some money on me for Whitsun, so that I may have a necklace. When the queen was here, I borrowed my cousin Elizabeth

Clere's things, because I was too ashamed to appear in beads among so many pretty ladies as were here then.

'The blessed Trinity have you in his keeping. Written at Norwich on the Friday before St George's day.'

By yours, M. Paston

The queen was probably seeking to arrange a match between Elizabeth Clere and one of her retinue; we find the earl of Oxford writing to John Paston about this time with the same purpose in mind:

'*Right trusty and right entirely well-beloved*, we greet you with all our heart. As you well know, we have Thomas Denys in our service, and have had him for a long time, and hoped that he would continue to attend on us at our pleasure. But on close examination of his behaviour, we feel certain that the love and affection he has for a lady not far from you, and which you know about (so we believe), causes him to long to be in your part of the country, rather than carrying out his duties for us. So we are writing to you asking you earnestly for our sake to do what you can at our request, by whatever means seem wise to you, to persuade that lady on our behalf to resolve this matter for the best. You may undertake that we will be generous to them both if she is ready to agree to this proposal, so that if she is reasonable she ought to be pleased by it. And if she would like us to come in person, we will do that and more, so we ask you to do your best, as we shall for you in future, and to come and see us quickly.

'The Holy Trinity keep you. Written at Wivenhoe on May 17.'

The earl of Oxford

Denys won his lady, only to meet with a series of disasters: he was imprisoned for a brawl between his hired man and one Walter Ingham to whom his wife owed money, and his wife, too, was imprisoned soon afterwards. Clearly, Denys had done something serious, for the earl of Oxford had turned against him; his enemies claimed that Denys forged a summons from the earl in order to lure him into an ambush, and if this was true it would explain the earl's change of heart. This was in 1454; but although his enemies got a bill against him in the Lords, it was rejected in the Commons.

John Paston seems to have supported him consistently through his troubles: there are three letters to him from Denys in the Fleet Prison, in which Denys bewails his fate, signing one letter 'written in no ease of heart in the Fleet on May 4, woeful Denys'.

Paston wrote frankly to the earl of Oxford in March 1454, less on behalf of Denys than of his wife. He reminds the earl how Agnes Denys had been imprisoned, even though pregnant, at the instigation of Cardinal Kemp and the earl himself, 'and is still daily vexed and troubled, as are her servants, to the total ruin of her person and goods.' He continues:

'In which, my lord, for reverence of God, remember that she was married by you, and by means of me on your written instructions. In the beginning she was very much against the match; she was worth 500 marks or more, and could have had a gentleman of this county who owned 100 marks of land and was of good birth, if it had not been for your influence and your letter to me. In consideration of this, in your wisdom and discretion, I trust, my lord, that you will help her, though she was imprisoned by other men's devices. If she is ruined by this marriage, I think in all conscience that I am bound to recompense her as far as my humble means will allow.'

Paston admits that Thomas Denys has offended the earl and behaved very unwisely 'and it is right that his person should be punished as it pleases you', and repeats his plea that the lady is only in trouble because of the earl's urging of the match. She seems to have been released soon afterwards, and Denys emerged from prison within a year or so. But in 1461, when he was coroner of Norfolk, he was attacked by allies of Paston's old enemy Heydon. He had to escape from his own house when the 'governor' of Norwich sent men to search for him. And once more he turned to John Paston for help:

'But I beg you to continue to be my master, and to give my wife help and comfort in her trouble; for were it not for her, God knows, I would soon settle matters. Truly I have no thought nor sorrow except for her. So I beg of you, for his love who succours and sustains us all, to show favour to her and comfort her. It will not be long before I send her a message telling her where to go.'

Denys took refuge at court, but found little comfort there. In May 1461 he wrote from York to John Paston describing his attempts to win favour: After reminding him of what had happened, Denys says:

'Here in the king's house, as far as Howard is concerned, whom I hoped might help me, I have been supplanted and rejected by him because all his followers clamoured for him to do so; but apparently he does not agree with my view of things anyway, so I am less worried. I do not want to compete if bribery is likely to be used; otherwise this unfortunate unkindness would, I think, have killed me.

'Please, for reverence of Jesus Christ, tell my lord of Warwick about me. By God, I have served him well. I was with him at Northampton, as everyone knows; and again recently at St Albans, as James Ratcliff knows, and lost £20 of harness and money, and was wounded in various places. . .

'Please write to me by the next man who comes from you. I would come to you, but, so help me God, I cannot afford it.

'The Holy Trinity preserve you. Written in haste at York. Yours to the best of his ability.'

Denys

But Denys did not get the protection he so badly needed. In early July 1461 he was back in Norfolk, and was abducted from his house by a gang led by the parson of Snoring, who murdered him. In such troubled times it was a matter of life and death to win a great lord's favour.

However, we have digressed from the Pastons themselves, whom we left in the uneasy peace of 1453. Margaret Paston's letters at this time are concerned with nothing more serious than household matters.

15 October, 1453

'*Right worshipful husband,* I commend myself to you, begging that you will not be angry with me, even though my stupidity caused you to be so. On my word of honour I do not want to do or say anything that would make you angry, and if I have done I am sorry and will make amends for it. So please forgive me and do not bear a grudge against me, for your anger would be hard for me to bear.

'I am sending the roll of parchment that you sent previously, sealed up, by the bearer of this: it was found in your travelling chest. As to herring, I have bought a horseload for 4s 6d: that is all I can get at the moment. I am promised some beaver, but cannot get it yet.

'I sent a message to Joan Petch about the windows, because she could not come to me, and she answered that she had spoken about it to Thomas Ingham. He said he would speak to you himself and come to an agreement. He said that she should not ask him to block the window-openings; and he said in any case that he could not do it, because he only leases the place. As for all the other errands that you have ordered me to do, they shall be done as soon as possible.

'The blessed Trinity have you in his keeping. Written at Norwich on the Monday after St Edward.'

Yours, M.P.

The errands were not all on one side: Margaret sent a good list for her husband in November.

'As for cloth for my gown, I cannot get anything better than the sample I am sending you, which is, I think, too poor both in cloth and colour, so please buy me 3¼ yards of whatever you think is suitable for me, of what colour you like, for I have really searched all the drapers' shops in this town, and there is a very poor choice. Please buy a loaf of good sugar as well, and half a pound of whole cinnamon, for there is no good cinnamon in this town.'

At the beginning of 1454, Margaret was evidently involved in the re-building of part of the house at Norwich, and her letter about progress of the work gives a few glimpses of the arrangement of the house:

'Thomas Howes has got four great beams for the private room and the malthouse and the brewery, three of which he has bought: the fourth, which will be the longest and largest of all, he will get from Hellesdon; he says that Fastolf will give it to me, because it is to be used to build my room. As to the laying of these beams, they will be laid this coming week because of the malthouse; as to the rest of the work, I think it must wait until you come home because I cannot get either joists or boards yet. I have measured the private room where you want your chests and accounting-board to be kept for the time being, and there is no room beside the bed, even if it was moved to the door, to put both your board and chests and to have space to move and sit down as well. So I have arranged that you shall have the same private room as you had before, and you will sleep there alone, and when your things are taken out of your little house, the door shall be locked and your bags laid in one of the great chests, where I hope they will be safe.'

Another letter probably dates from this period; in it Margaret asks her husband that 'if you have another son that you will let it be named Henry in memory of your brother Henry' and signs herself 'your groaning wife', so she was evidently expecting another child shortly. It is the last of her letters to John for over five years; the series resumes in 1459. Either a bundle of her letters was lost, or John was more frequently at home; the latter is possible, as in about 1454 he became legal adviser to Sir John Fastolf of Caister Castle, Margaret's neighbour at her home at Mautby and possibly a relation of hers. From Fastolf's letters to him, John was clearly much more occupied with local business than in the past. He was also concerned once more with the longstanding problem of a marriage for his sister Elizabeth, for whose hand there were various offers. John Clopton, who had been sheriff of Norfolk and Suffolk two years earlier, seems to have almost agreed terms with John Paston and his mother in April 1454; a draft settlement was drawn up, granting Elizabeth 400 marks on her marriage, and John's father was to give the couple lands worth £40 a year. Why the negotiations broke down at this late stage we do not know; instead, we have correspondence with an even higher-ranking suitor. Edward Lord Gray wrote to John on July 11;

'Trusty and well-beloved friend, I commend myself to you, and wish to tell you that if your sister is not yet married, I trust to God that I know how she may be married to a gentleman with an income of 300 marks a year, a great man by birth and of good family. If you think you can negotiate anything in this connection please send me word by the bringer of this letter, because I have spoken to those concerned and they have agreed to proceed no further until I speak to them again. So please send me word quickly what your attitude to this will be.'

Paston replied politely, but without committing himself, four days later:

'. . . indeed, my lord, she is neither married nor promised to anyone. There are, and have been, at various times recently, approaches about such a marriage from various gentlemen, but these are not settled as yet; whether the gentleman your lordship has in mind is one of them or not I cannot tell. As for the request in your letter that I should send you word whether I thought you should proceed in the matter or not, I dare not presume to write and say unless I know the gentleman's name.'

John Paston goes on to say that he is prepared to promise that his sister will not be promised or married to anyone within the next month, to give Lord Gray time to send details of the proposed bridegroom. Between the lines, we can perhaps read some suspicion on John's part; if so, he was justified, as a letter from his young brother William was to prove. William had been at Cambridge until quite recently, but was in London during the summer, where he was able to send useful information to his brother. In conversation with Thomas Billing, a sergeant-at-law, he discovered Lord Gray's purpose in proposing the match:

'. . . he asked me how my sister was and I said she was well and never been better than now. He said he was with Lord Gray and they talked about a gentleman who was a ward of his lordship – I remember that he said it was Harry Gray whom they talked of. And my lord said, "I have just been trying in these last few days to marry him to a lady in Norfolk who will have 400 marks when she marries; but I will not do it for him, because I could have done with 400 marks, and now he wants the marriage money himself: and so," he said, "he can make his own marriage." These were my lord's words to Billing, or so he said. He understood that my lord was trying to organise things to his own advantage, and advised me to tell her to be cautious. And I thanked him for his good advice.

'I send you an answer to your letter about when Sir John Fastolf was coming home, and reported what he told me himself. Nevertheless, he stayed longer than he said he was going to. He told me he would arrange things between Scrope and my sister while he was in Norfolk. Many people do not want it to happen, because they say it is an unsuitable marriage. If there is any more talk of Cressener, he is said to be a gentleman, and of good reputation. You know who is of good repute better than I do. For God's sake, get matters settled; it is high time.'

Matters of state soon overshadowed such domestic affairs. In August 1453, Henry VI had a mental breakdown, and the duke of York emerged as protector of the realm. He attempted to reconcile the courtiers who had long opposed him by including their leaders in his administration, but the rival factions were now too deeply divided for this to solve the problem. What had in effect happened during the period of Henry VI's minority was that the type of rivalries and local struggles for power we have already observed in the Paston territory of Norfolk were repeated on both a lesser and greater scale across the country. The relative stability of the nobility in the late thirteenth and early fourteenth century had given way under Richard II and Henry VI to a situation where great territorial power could be built up rapidly at the king's whim, and as rapidly destroyed. The new men were creatures of the court, challenging the old-fashioned regional families. The most striking case of this was the rivalry between the Nevills and Percys in northern England. The Nevills, who had first risen to importance in Richard II's reign, when Ralph Nevill was created first earl of Westmorland, were in this case the newcomers, deliberately encouraged by Richard as a counterbalance to the over-mighty Percy earls of Northumberland. Ralph Nevill's twelve children all made important marriages, his eldest son becoming earl of Salisbury, and the pattern was repeated in the next generation, when Richard Nevill married the heiress of the earl of Warwick, and so acquired the title and the great Beauchamp estates that went with it. The Percys resisted this burgeoning dynasty as best they could, and in 1443–4, the enmity between the two became open warfare, which the duke of York tried, rather ineffectually, to suppress.

In the spring of 1454, someone in John Paston's entourage, perhaps Paston himself, drew up a petition to the newly-appointed protector which showed that even when no great political disturbance was afoot, there was great disorder in the countryside. The petition is concerned with the activities of Robert Ledham, who had been responsible with others for the death of Philip Berney, Margaret Paston's uncle, as a result of wounds received in an ambush. The writer paints a vivid picture of the countryside being terrorised by a gang:

'. . .the said Robert Ledham, with his fellow-rioters committed so many riots in the hundred where he lived that many gentlemen, freeholders and good men did not dare to stay in their houses nor ride or walk about their business without more persons equipped for war in attendance on them than their income allowed them to afford. So, in order to save their lives and avoid such inordinate costs, the like of which were never seen in that county before, many of them forsook their own dwellings, their wives and children, and withdrew to fortresses and safe towns for the time being.'

However, John's standing in the county was high, and William Paston gives an interesting picture of him from a mutual acquaintance which shows what his reputation was at this time:

'*Right worshipful brother*, I commend myself to you: as for news, my lord of York has taken my lord of Exeter into his custody. The duke of Somerset is still in prison, in a worse state than he was.

'Sir John Fastolf asks to be remembered to you. He is going to Norfolk on Thursday, and will stay at Caister, and Scrope with him. He says that you are the truest kinsman and friend that he knows. He would like to have you living at Mautby.

'Billing made me very welcome on the way, and he told me privately what he said to Ledham. Ledham wanted advice about making a complaint to Prisot in the shire court about you, and Billing advised him to forget it, telling Ledham that he was not going to associate with him. He said to Ledham: "Your companions in the country like to spend all they have on men and liveries and horses and harness, and live like that for a time, and in the end they are beggars; and that is what will happen to you. I would like you to prosper, because you are a fellow of Gray's Inn, where I was a fellow myself. As for Paston, he is a gentleman of great reputation, and with a good income; and I know that he does not spend all he has at once, but saves a hundred marks or a hundred pounds a year. He can do much harm to his enemies, and yet not be worse off, either in his household or in the number of men he has with him. You could not do this except perhaps for a year or so. My advice is not to continue your lawsuit as long as you are doing, and to make peace with Paston." And I thanked Billing on your behalf.

'God have you in his keeping.'

By your poor brother William Paston

'I could tell you much else if I had time. Remember me to my sister-in-law Margaret and my cousin Elizabeth Clere, please.'

John's influence in the county was recognised by no less than the duke of York himself in August, when he and his nephew by marriage, Richard earl of Warwick, wrote about two manors which the earl had bought at Walsingham, Warwick's letter ran:

'*Worshipful and my right trusty and well-beloved friend*, I greet you well. Inasmuch as I have purchased from my worshipful and well-beloved friend the prior of Walsingham two manors in Little Snoring, with the appurtenances, I desire and ask you with all my heart to show to me and my feoffees your goodwill and favour, so that through your friendship I may enjoy the aforesaid purchase all the more peaceably.

'Please believe what my well-beloved chaplain Sir John Southwell, bearer of this letter, has to say about this matter, and be a true friend to me, since I trust you greatly; by doing this you will give me a great pleasure, and I will be your patron, and will be of assistance to you at some time, by the grace of God; may he preserve you and send you good health.

'Given under my signet at Middleham on August 23.'

R. Warwick

From this and other details in the letters, it is clear that John Paston was a supporter of the Yorkist cause, as one might expect. In broad terms, the Yorkists stood for those opposed to the courtiers who had surrounded Henry VI for so many years; they wanted a return to good government, and were generally the conservative, established county gentlemen, who had everything to gain from peace in the country and the suppression of the intrigues round the king. For the moment, they had the upper hand, but it was not to last. In February 1455, Henry VI recovered his sanity, and the Protectorate was brought to an end. With the king's restoration to power, the pendulum swung to the other extreme. Margaret of Anjou, his queen, had been denied the Protec-torate by the Lords, who had preferred York; she had therefore allied herself with York's most extreme enemies, and now began to take her revenge. It was increasingly clear that the struggle was not merely for political power, but for the succession to the throne, and Margaret was anxious to secure this for her young son Prince Edward, which meant that York, as the next and most powerful claimant, had to be eliminated from the political scene. York's reply to her actions was to rearm, and although a settlement by negotiation was tried, talks broke down. Both sides gathered supporters and put armies in the field, though York was better prepared. The armies met at St Albans on May 22, and after a relatively brief fight, York's troops emerged vic-torious. John Paston learnt of the battle a few days later, from an acquaintance, possibly a servant of his mother:

'*Right worshipful and most well-beloved sir*, I commend myself to you desiring with all my heart to hear how you are. This is to let you know that the news we have here is that three lords are dead: the duke of Somerset, the earl of Northumberland and Lord Clifford; as for any other well-known men I know of none except Watton of Cambridge-shire. As for the other lords, many of them are hurt; as for Feningley, he is alive and well, as far as I can find out.

'As for the general news of people there, as far as we can tell there were only a hundred and twenty killed at most. As for the lords who were with the king, they and their men were pillaged and robbed of their harness and horses. As for the kind of government we shall have now, I do not know, except that certain appointments have been made. My lord of York is constable of England, my lord of Warwick is captain of Calais, my Lord Bourchier is treasurer of England; and I have no other news yet. As for our sovereign lord, God be thanked, he is not badly hurt.'

The same day, Fastolf, writing to John about a lawsuit, added as a post-script: 'I trust to God that as the world is going now, this will all go well, with your help'; things looked favourable once again. York's full ascendancy did not last for long, however. In February 1456, he was discharged from the protectorship, and Margaret of Anjou resumed control. Although she took care not to offend the Yorkists for the moment, the misgovernment of Henry's earlier years returned. The men in charge of the administration developed a system whereby the court could draw directly on revenue collected by the sheriffs, thus avoiding the control of both treasury and parliament. Among this court party was Paston's old enemy Sir Thomas Tuddenham; and with the duke of York apparently reconciled to the courtiers, intrigues became even more devious than before: even in 1455, Paston wrote, in reply to a proposal to impeach Tuddenham and Heydon that 'Tuddenham has given me no cause recently to plot against him,' though he was keen to proceed against Heydon. At the local level, alliances shifted and old quarrels were made up, according to the success of individual factions rather than in harmony with national policies.

We have no letters written by the Pastons between July 1455 and May 1458, though many letters to them survive, mostly business letters from Sir John Fastolf and his secretaries. John Paston was appointed justice of the peace in 1456-7, and this seems to have been a very busy period in his life, but also a period singularly free from personal lawsuits and problems. He managed to solve one longstanding headache, by arranging the marriage of his sister Elizabeth to Robert Poynings. We have a letter from her to her mother, Agnes, soon after her marriage, which seems to have taken place in the autumn of 1458. After an obsequious opening, perhaps written with a memory of those earlier beatings in mind, she continues:

'As for my master, my best-beloved as you call him – and as I ought to call him now, because I find no reason not to, and as I trust in Jesus, never shall – he is very kind to me and is as busy as he can to make sure of my marriage settlement, for which he is bound by a bond of £1000 to you, mother, and to my brother, John, and to my brother William, and to Edmund Clere, even though such a bond was unnecessary.'

She goes on, however, to ask her mother to make sure that she pays the money promised as dowry when it is due, as her husband needs to pay off an old debt, and also asks that Lady Pole with whom she lived in London before her marriage, should be paid for her trouble. Clearly, Poynings' credit was not so good, and the bond was a wise precaution on John's part: Poynings had been involved in Cade's rebellion, and although he had influential friends, was perhaps not the ideal match, but the best that John could manage after all the years of fruitless negotiations. Agnes herself was evidently more concerned about Clement, her fourth son, now under a tutor in London, if a note about errands to be done in London in January 1458 is anything to go by:

'Grenefeld to send word faithfully in writing whether Clement Paston has done his duty in learning. If he has not done well, and will not try harder, ask him to beat him severely until he does. His last master at Cambridge, the best he ever had, did so. Tell Grenefeld that if he will undertake to make him behave and learn properly, so that I know he is doing his duty, I will give him 10 marks for his trouble; for I would rather he was buried than lost for want of trying. Item, see how many gowns Clement has; have the worn ones brushed to bring up the nap. He has a short green gown and a short grey gown that have not been brushed up, and a short blue gown that was brushed up and made into a side gown when I was last in London, a russet side gown furred with beaver made this time two years ago, and a purple side gown made this time twelve months ago.

'Item, have made for me six spoons of eight ounces troy weight, well made and double-gilt.

'Tell Elizabeth Paston that she must accustom herself to working as readily as other gentlewomen do, and so help herself.

'Item, pay Lady Pole 26s 8d for her board.

'And if Grenefeld has done his duty with Clement, or will do this duty, give him a noble.'

John Paston was now preoccupied with the administration of Fastolf's estates. Fastolf was now an old man, and in poor health, and relied increasingly on John's services. John acted as his chief adviser and lawyer, with a small group of secretaries among whom was William Worcester, later famous for his topographical writings, the *Itineraries*, one of the first attempts to survey the notable sights of England. Another adviser was Thomas Howes, parson of Blofield, whose signature appears jointly with that of Paston on a letter in May 1458. At this time, Fastolf's main concern, besides the routine administration of his estates was the establishment of a college of priests at Caister Castle, arrangements for which began to be made in 1456. They were still not completed in the autumn of 1459, when Friar John Brackley, a member of Fastolf's household, wrote to John Paston

'*Right reverend master*, come as soon as you can to Caister, and Yelverton with you, if you can arrange it; and send home your horses and man until you have finished here. And by the grace of God and by your wisdom and policy you can bring some very substantial matters to a conclusion, to the praise and profit of your master and yourself. It is high time. He is going fast to his home, and is very low, much weakened and enfeebled. You must bring with you a form of supplication drawn up in London setting out how master R. Popy, a knowledgeable and skilled man, shall present and plead before the king for the amortising of Caister to St Benet, which he promised to do for a certain sum, and undertook it, and at the time made no bones about the matter. And he says now that he will do everything necessary; and he wants me to help him, which cannot be, or else a trustworthy man of my masters (I doubt if this can be arranged). God bring you here soon, for I am weary of waiting.

'Sir Thomas, the parson, and I have not discussed the matter any further with my master. Every day for the past five days he has said "God send me soon my good cousin Paston, for I think he is a man of his word and a man of integrity." I replied: "That is true," and he answered, "Don't show me the meat, show me the man." These words he repeats often, with great impatience.'

On November 5, Sir John died, having made a new will two days previously. In it, he repeated his longstanding intention to found a college of priests at Caister, consisting of seven 'religious men, monks or secular priests and seven poor folk, to pray for his soul and the souls of his wife, father and mother and others to whom he was beholden, in perpetuity.' As he had not been able to establish it himself, he entrusted John Paston with this task. John, within a reasonable time of Sir John's decease, was to make arrangements for the college and provide it with a suitable income. In return for this and a payment of 4000 marks to be used by his executors for masses for the souls of those already mentioned, John Paston was to inherit the whole of the Fastolf lands. A later amendment on November 4, released John from the payment of 4000 marks. John and Thomas Howes were named as the effective executors, and a curious proviso was added, that John was to pull down Caister if he was prevented from founding the college there 'by force or might of anyone else desiring to have the said mansion'. Fastolf had already been approached by the duchess of York about the purchase of Caister, and he knew that others would be interested, as time was to show.

It was one thing for John Paston to be named as heir, quite another for him to make good his claim, particularly since the relative peace of the past three years had been shattered earlier in the year. The earl of Warwick, who had made Calais a powerful Yorkist base, was conducting his own diplomacy on the continent, in conflict with that of Queen Margaret, and during the summer of 1459 it became clear that a new confrontation was imminent. The Yorkists moved first, Warwick returned to England, and moved towards Warwickshire, while his father, the earl of Salisbury, defeated the Lancastrians at Blore Heath on September 23, before the whole Yorkist force assembled at Ludlow. But on October 12, at Ludford Bridge, the Yorkist army was dispersed; and York and Warwick fled to Ireland and Calais respectively. On November 20 all the Yorkist lords were formally attainted in parliament of treason.

In the midst of such turmoil, it may seem extraordinary that any government business could be carried on; but William Paston was able to report some initial success in the great objective that was to occupy the family for the next decade. In a letter on November 12, just a week after Fastolf's death:

'*Right well-beloved brother*, I commend myself to you. This is to inform

75

you that on the morning of last Friday, Worcester and I came to London by eight o'clock; we spoke to the lord chancellor, and I found him well-disposed in every way, and you will find him a very profitable friend. And he asked me to write to you a letter in his name, and entrusted you with gathering together all the goods, asking you to do this and to get all his goods out of every place of his, his own place included, wherever they are, and to lay them up secretly as you think best and arrange accordingly, until he speaks to you himself; and he said that you should have all such favour as was lawful. I intend to ride to him today to get writs of *diem clausit extremum* [for an inquest into lands held by the deceased] and I expect you will get a letter from him. As for the goods in St Paul's, they are safe enough, and today we have got a grant for the goods from Bermondsey without anyone knowing except Worcester, Plomer and myself; and no one shall know of it except the three of us.

'My lord treasurer speaks as if he were a friend, but many people warn me not to trust him. Many men are plotting to prove the king's right to all his [Fastolf's] goods. Southwell is the escheator, and he is a good friend and well disposed. My lord Exeter claims title in my master's place in Southwark with the appurtenances, and indeed intended to make an entry. His counsel were with us, and spoke to Worcester and me, and have now sent word that they will urge his lordship to sue by legal means. I have spoken to the archbishop of Canterbury and Master John Stokes, and find them both very well disposed. . .

'As for William Worcester, he hopes that you will do what you can for him and for his benefit, within reason, and I am sure that if he is certain that you intend to do this you will find him faithful. I understood from him that he wants no other master after his old master, and in my opinion it would be a pity if he did not benefit from my master to the extent that he need never take up service again, considering how my master trusted him, the long years he was with him, and the many difficult journeys he made for his sake.

'This is all for now, because you will get another letter tomorrow. Written at London on November 12 in haste.'

By William Paston

A month later, Fastolf's old servant John Bokkyng reported from the parliament meeting at Coventry; although Fastolf's will was one topic of concern, he was now concerned lest any of Fastolf's or Paston's men, including John Paston himself, should be named in the bills of attainder against the Yorkists which parliament was drawing up. All was well, however, and none of them were named, though they were evidently well-known by now as Yorkist supporters.

On Christmas eve, Margaret wrote to John with a different problem, one of etiquette. What was the correct procedure at Christmas in a great household in mourning? She had taken advice, however, and was fairly confident of what was required:

'*Right worshipful husband*, I commend myself to you. This is to let you know that I sent your eldest son to Lady Morley to find out what entertainment was put on in her house the Christmas after the death of her husband. And she said that there were no disguisings or harping or lute-playing or singing, and no noisy amusements, but backgammon and chess and cards; these were the games she allowed her people to play, and no others. Your son did his errand very well, as you will hear later. I sent your younger son to Lady Stapleton, and she said the same as Lady Morley, adding that this was what they did in respectable houses that she had been to.

'Please try to get someone at Caister to keep the buttery, for the man who you left with them will not make up the account daily, as you ordered. He says that he has not been used to giving an account either of the bread or of the ale until the end of the week, and he says that he knows he cannot do it; so I think that he had better not stay. And I think you would be glad to get another man instead of Simon, for you are none the closer to a sensible man with him.

'I am sorry you will not be home at Christmas; please come as soon as you can. I shall feel half a widow because you will not be there. God have you in his keeping. Written on Christmas eve.'

By your M.P.

Early in 1460, the first sign of difficulty over Fastolf's will appeared. William Paston's hopes of getting the writs of *diem clausit extremum* issued quickly, so that the executors' work could begin, were disappointed: they were not issued until May 1460, and the necessary inquests were delayed until October. More serious, Fastolf's old servants began to turn against John Paston. At some time between the end of November 1459 and early January 1460, Worcester quarrelled with John Paston: he had clearly had high expectations of reward under his master's will, and had told local people in Norfolk that he was to be one of the chief executors. Now he found himself merely one of the eight advisory executors, and, furthermore, without any specific inheritance. In a letter to a friend, he claimed that Fastolf had granted him lands before his death, but that Thomas Howes, his wife's uncle and the other chief executor, would not acknowledge his claim, even though he had been present when Fastolf promised them:

'My master too ... granted me a livelihood suitable to my standing, so that I, my wife and my children should have cause to pray for him. My wife's uncle was present in his chapel at Caister, as well as my wife, and he commanded her uncle to choose the lands. This is true, by the blessed sacrament that I received at Easter. And because I demanded my rights and dues from Master Paston, he is not pleased. I have lost more than ten marks worth of land in my master's service, by God, and unless I am compensated the whole world shall know how I am wronged.'

Writing to one of Margaret Paston's relations, John Berney, at this time, Worcester had further complaints to make:

'*Right worshipful sir*, I commend myself to you. The reason why I have come to London and am staying here is because I undertook by my letters to be here now and settle up with all the creditors with whom I made my master's friends (God bless his soul) stand surety for me for the cloth I had bought for my master's burial. I only held the candle among you in Norfolk, because I was not in such favour or trust as to order or give in my master's name, a cloth for a gown to his friends, servants of almspeople, but had to beg and pray as if I were a stranger. If I caused Master Paston and my uncle the parson to have such authority as they now enjoy, they ought to be all the more glad and eager to continue my authority, which is as great as theirs or greater, whatever Friar Brackley or they say, and it is on public record as well.'

On January 28, William Paston and Thomas Playter reported again to John from London. The Pastons' newly acquired fortune had aroused jealousy even among old friends: there were charges that the will of November 3 was a forgery, made after Fastolf's death, and even William Yelverton was now hostile. Thomas Playter regarded Worcester as a more serious nuisance, however, and wanted to compromise.

'William Worcester came to London two days before we came, but we cannot find any obvious signs that he is plotting, nor can we hear or discover any secret plans of his; for I, Playter, had a conversation with him, and he says nothing at all, except that he wants to be rewarded for his long and faithful service of his master's estate as his master promised during his lifetime. And whenever I said to him that it cannot be denied that, as to all his master's land in Norfolk and Suffolk, it was his will, sufficiently proven, that you should have it, he answered by asking me to say no more about it, because he knows nothing of a [. . .] covenant, and I cannot get anything more out of him. But, before God, I feel that he could help us to get hold of a thousand or two thousand marks which we could not obtain without his help, as he claims. And to see whether he was lying or speaking the truth, I asked him if he would take as his reward anything we could not get without his help, and he said yes, willingly, so think about it.'

Four months later, John Bokkyng, another of Fastolf's clerks, was also hostile; William Paston reported on May 2.

'I spoke to Bokkyng today. He said little, but I felt from what he said that he was very hostile to the parson [Howes] and you; but he spoke very guardedly. . . I gather that Bokkyng and Worcester put great trust in their own simple ideas, whatever these may mean. Bokkyng told me today that he was as high in my master Fastolf's opinion four days before he died as any man in England. I said I thought not – perhaps that this was true three years before his death. I told him that I had heard various things he was reported to have said, and I did not think that they would be easily brought about; and he swore that he had talked to no one about anything against your interests. It is he who is making William Worcester so troublesome. I wish you had a statement from Robert Inglose, even if only to say that my master was in his right mind, because he was so recently with my master Fastolf. Worcester said at Caister that it would be necessary for you to have good witnesses and said that things would go hard with you if your witnesses were not more than adequate.'

John had already realised that witnesses were badly needed to a will that had been made at the last minute in favour of those at the knight's deathbed. Already, in January, he had obtained a letter from Geoffrey Sperlyng describing a conversation with Fastolf in which the latter had outlined his intentions; and three years later he was still collecting such testimonies from Yarmouth men to whom Fastolf had declared his plans for the disposal of the estates.

But politics at large were once again overshadowing even such great matters as the disposal of the Fastolf lands. In the early summer of 1460, probably as part of a government witch-hunt of Yorkist supporters, John Paston, his uncle by marriage, John Berney, and others were accused of robbery. Within the next two months, however, the political situation was once more totally reversed. On June 26, the Yorkists invaded once again, and London opened its gates to them, only the Tower holding out. On July 10, the Yorkist army commanded by the earls of March and Warwick – York himself was still in Ireland – met the king's army near Northampton and won a decisive victory, capturing the king. A parliament was summoned for October 7, and John Paston attended it as MP for Norfolk. Its prime object was to reverse the sentences of attainder passed on the Yorkist nobles in the parliament of 1459; but the duke of York had other plans as well. He arrived at Westminster on October 10, having made it plain that he intended to claim the throne. This clearly dismayed his supporters; when he arrived, he went up to the empty throne and briefly stood by it, expecting acclamation: there was only silence. The archbishop of Canterbury broke it by asking him if he wished to see the king. York replied: 'I know of no one in the realm who would not more fitly come to me than I to him,' and six days later made a formal claim in writing to the throne, claiming it by hereditary right.

But York had misjudged the mood of his supporters: no one wanted a change of dynasty at that moment, and the eventual settlement agreed was that Henry should have the throne for his lifetime; York was to be his heir. His triumph was short-lived; in a minor skirmish outside Wakefield on December 30, he was killed when attacking a much larger Lancastrian force led by the duke of Somerset and the earl of Northumberland.

John Paston was away from home from early October onwards, and so missed the vital inquests on Fastolf's lands, held at Acle on October 18 and Bungay on October 30; but Margaret kept him informed of matters, helped by their two eldest sons, both named after John. John III acted as his mother's secretary about this time, and his elder brother was helping with the administration of the estates, at one point searching unsuccessfully through the three large canvas bags in his father's 'great standing chest' for a copy of a document. On 23 January 1461 Clement, John I's brother wrote to him warning him to prepare for war, following the death of York at Wakefield; Lord Fitzwalter had just left for the north.

'Whatever he is told by the lords who are here, it would be as well for you to see that the men of the county are always ready to come, both footmen and horsemen, when they are sent for; for I have heard it said that the more distant lords will be here sooner than men think, I have heard it said before three weeks are out. Also you should come with more men and better equipped than anyone else in the county, because it is for the good of your reputation and you are more involved than other men of that county; and you are more in favour with the lords here. Here everyone is ready to go with the lords, and I hope God will help them, for the people in the north rob and steal and have arranged to pillage all this part of the world, and to give away men's goods and livelihood throughout the south, and that will stir up trouble. The lords who are here have as much as they can do to keep this part of the world under control, because they want to attack the northerners, for the good of everyone in the south.'

Events followed rapidly in the next month. The earl of March won a victory at Mortimer's Cross in Herefordshire on February 3, but Warwick was defeated at the second battle of St Albans on February 17, and Queen Margaret regained control of the king. But she failed to gain London, which was back in the control of Warwick and March on February 27. For a brief period the Lancastrians seemed to be in the ascendant again, and on March 1 Margaret wrote to John warning him of dangers if he returned to Norfolk.

'This is to let you know that I am informed by someone who is well-disposed towards you that an ambush is being prepared for you in this county if you come here openly, to take you to the presence of a certain lord in the north, which will not be comfortable for you, but will put you in danger of your life or of great and serious loss of your goods. The man who has undertaken this enterprise was under-sheriff to G. Sayntlowe; he is in great favour here, through the son of William Baxter who lies buried at Greyfriars [i.e. Heydon]. And, so it is reported, the son has given much money to the lords in the north to bring this about, and now he and all his old fellowship preen their plumage and are high-spirited and merry, hoping that everything is and will be as they would have it. I am also told that the father of the bastard [i.e. Tuddenham] said in these parts that the shire would be made safe for him and his heirs from now on, and for the Baxters' heirs as well; from which I believe that they think they have no enemy other than you. So please be all the more cautious how you go and watch for your safety; and do not be in too much of a hurry to come to these parts until you hear that things are safer. I think the bearer of this can tell you more, by word of mouth, as far as he knows of it, of the state of affairs here.

'God have you in his keeping. Written in haste the second Sunday of Lent, by candle-light in the evening.'

By yours, etc M.

The generally disturbed state of the county at this time is vividly portrayed in a letter from John III, probably sent to Thomas Playter.

'I commend myself to you; this is to let you know that notwithstanding the instructions sent, as you know, that people should not come up until they were sent for, but were to be ready at all times, many people from these parts have nonetheless enlisted, saying they will go up to London. But they have no captain or commander assigned by the commissioners under whom they can gather, and so they straggle about by themselves, and in all probability half of them are unlikely to get to London. And men who have come from London say that no more than four hundred have got past Thetford, and yet the towns and the county who have paid their wages will think they have done their duty. So if the lords wait for more men from these parts, it will not be easy to get them without a new commission and summons; and yet those who have paid wages for men will think it very strange to have to pay more men, for every town has paid wages for and sent out, or are ready to send out, as many as they did when the king sent for them before the battle at Ludlow, and those who have not gone are going in the same disorderly fashion.

'There was serious trouble here, for a certain person, after the battle at Wakefield, gathered a company to murder John Damme, it is said, and there are also at Castle Rising and two other places great gatherings of men and hiring of harness, and it is clearly understood that they are not for the king, but rather the contrary, and for robbery.'

But the Yorkist party were not dispirited by their reverses. The step which they had refused to take under the duke of York's leadership, of setting up a rival claimant to the crown, was taken in favour of his son, Edward, earl of March, who on March 4 was proclaimed and recognised as Edward IV by the citizens of London. Nine days later he set out to find the Lancastrian army, meeting them at Towton in Yorkshire on March 24. The battle was a long and hard one, finally decided in Edward's favour by the arrival of fresh troops, the East Anglian contingent under the duke of Norfolk, who had not been able to catch up with the main army on the march north.

Five days after the battle, William Paston reported the victory to John as follows:

'You will be pleased to know the news my lady of York had in a letter of credence signed by our sovereign lord King Edward, which reached her today, Easter Eve, at eleven o'clock, and was seen and

83

read by me William Paston. First, our sovereign lord has won the campaign, and on the Monday after Palm Sunday he was received in York with great solemnity and processions. And the mayor and commons contrived to have his grace through Lord Montagu and Lord Berners, who, before the king came into the city, asked him for grace for the said city, which he granted them.

'On the king's side Lord Fitzwalter was killed, and Lord Scrope badly hurt. John Stafford and Horne of Kent are dead, and Humphrey Stafford and William Hastings made knights, among others; Blunt is knighted. On the other side Lord Clifford, Lord Neville, Lord Wells, Lord Willoughby, Anthony Lord Scales, Lord Harry and apparently, the earl of Northumberland, Andrew Trollop and many other gentlemen and commoners, to the number of 20,000, are dead.

'King Henry, the queen, the prince of Wales, the duke of Somerset, the duke of Exeter and Lord Roos have fled into Scotland, and they are being chased and followed. We did not send word to you before because we had no definite news; for until today London was as sad a city as it could be.'

Thomas Playter reported such further news as he had in London to John Paston on April 18:

'. . . as for news, it is rumoured (and said to be true by reputable men and others) that the earl of Wiltshire is taken, and Doctor Morton and Doctor Makerell, and they have been taken to the king at York. Master William spoke to a man who saw them.

'Sir, I heard from Sir John Borcester and Christopher Hanson that Henry the Sixth is in a place in Yorkshire called Corcumbre; that is its name, or something like it. The place is besieged, and various squires of the earl of Northumberland have gathered five or six thousand men to attack the besiegers, so that in the meantime Henry the Sixth could be smuggled out through a little postern gate on the other side: and four thousand men of the north were killed in this attack. Sir Robert of Acle and Conyers are laying siege to it on our side, and it was they that did this deed. Some say that the queen, Somerset and the prince of Wales are there.

'It is reported to be true that the earl of Northumberland is dead.

'The earl of Devonshire is indeed dead.

'My lord chancellor has gone to York.

'The king and the lords will not come here before Whitsun, it is said.

'As soon as the chief baron (of the exchequer) comes, I will send you a letter, by God's grace, who preserve you and have you in his blessed keeping.

Yours, Thomas Playter

'The earl of Wiltshire and the doctors were captured at Cockermouth.

'Some men say that Lord Wells, Willoughby and Scales are alive.

'Sir Robert Vere has been killed in Cornwall, it is reliably reported.'

The Yorkists were now firmly in the ascendant. Before Edward left York after Easter, a warrant for the arrest of Sir Thomas Tuddenham and others, 'rebels and adherents of King Henry VI' had been issued. The Pastons welcomed the victory, but it had not been achieved without cost: Robert Poynings, Elizabeth's husband, had been killed at St Albans, and her mother-in-law was trying to seize his lands. The revolution which had put Edward on the throne also meant a new series of civil disturbances: the first years of Edward's reign were perhaps worse than anything experienced under Henry, despite the king's own efforts to deal equitably with the contenders for his favour, and to uphold justice and order. John's standing with the new regime is emphasised by a letter from Thomas Playter early in June, saying that Edward was to be crowned on June 28.

'And John Jenney told me, and I have been assured of it since, that you are listed to be knighted at the coronation. Whether you have had prior notice of this, I do not know; but if you wish to take the title, considering the good news we have had and for the gladness and pleasure of all your wellwishers and to the pain and discomfort of all those who wish you harm, it is time that everything you need for it was got ready. And you will need to come to London, because I think that the knights are to be made on the Sunday before the coronation. Anything that can be got for you privately without expense I will obtain for you if necessary, in anticipation of your coming, hoping for the best. . .'

Nothing came of this, however, whether this was because John refused the honour or because it was not offered, we do not know. About the same time, a much more serious problem arose: the duke of Norfolk, who had long had his eye on Caister, and was rumoured to have bought it in November 1452, seized the castle and put in his men. Norfolk stood very high in the king's favour; his part at the battle of Towton had been decisive, and he was earl-marshal at the coronation. Yet Edward refused to act purely out of favouritism and John was able to obtain letters ordering Norfolk to release the castle. Richard Calle, the Pastons' bailiff, wrote to John on June 5, describing how he had tried to deliver the letters to the duke, but had failed. He said that there seemed to be two or three others in the plot including Fastolf's and Paston's former ward, Thomas Fastolf of Cowhaugh. The infamous John Heyson was at large again, and it was in the following month that Thomas Denys was murdered. As William Lomnor wrote on July 6, 'the world is right wild'. The wildness may not have all been on one side; at the elections for the shire, on June 15, John Paston and John Berney were returned, but there was great dispute about it, and the sheriff, Paston's enemy Sir John Howard, sent in a report accusing Paston's supporters of riotous behaviour and of uttering threats against those who opposed them. However, since Howard was subsequently involved in a brawl with John in the shire-house in August, and was eventually imprisoned in November because of the complaints against him, the report may have been malicious; Norfolk's men, who were probably responsible for the murder of Denys, had tried already to pin the blame for that crime on John Berney. One of Denys' last acts had been to send a report on the behaviour of the electors at the shire court in June to the king, presumably a version favourable to Paston and Berney. The skirmishes were not only physical, but were also waged in terms of propaganda. The election stood, after further intrigues, but Tuddenham, Heydon and their new ally Sir Miles Stapleton continued to cause trouble. John wrote to Margaret on July 12:

'And let him [John Berney] know that many complaints about him have been made by Sir Miles Stapleton, that knavish knight, as I sent you word before, but he will be able to clear himself easily enough if he has a man's courage, and Stapleton will be shown up for what he is, a deceitful intriguer. And he and his wife and others here spread gossip secretly about my family, but by the time we have taken into account the old days and today, my family will be found more reputable than his or his wife's, and I would not say otherwise even for a purse of gold from him. Also tell Berney that the sheriff is uncertain whether to hold a new election because of him and Grey, and it would be better for him to get the sheriff's favour over it.

'I think, for the sake of keeping the country quiet, the best way would be for Berney and Grey to get a record of everyone with 40s a year to spend who was at the election; whichever of them had the fewest votes from them should give up his claim... Written at London on Relic Sunday.

'Please send round for money according to the previous note I sent you from Lynn.

John Paston

Three days later Margaret wrote back to say that she had delivered the message, and that those responsible for Denys' death had been arrested, and on July 18 she requested John to try to get a commission of *oyer et terminer* to deal with the case; 'and as for the costs of it, the county will pay, for they are very much afraid that unless this death is punished... more people will be treated in the same way.'

Meanwhile John had sent his eldest son, John II, to court, in the hope that if he found favour there, he would be able to further the family's cause, particularly in the question of the Fastolf inheritance. On August 23, John Russe, an old servant of Fastolf and now employed by the Pastons, wrote to John saying that he had recently met a friend of his, John Waynfleet who had just come from court:

'And I asked him how my master your son was getting on, and he praised him greatly, saying that he had a good reputation, which grew daily, and that he was well known and liked among the gentlemen around the king. But he said that the only thing that might harm him was your restriction on the money you sent him, because unless he has enough money in his purse to spend a reasonable amount, they will set no store by him; and there are gentlemen's sons of less repute who

have ten times as much money to spend as he has. Waynfleet said that
you needed to remember this.'

Two days later, John's brother Clement also wrote about John II, giving a rather less optimistic report, based on news from John II's servant
Pekok:

'*Right reverend and worshipful brother*, I commend myself to you as a
brother, and hope to hear that you are well and prosperous. May God
increase your prosperity as he pleases, to your heart's ease. This is to
let you know that both I and Playter have spoken to John Russe on the
Friday before St Bartholomew. And he told us about Howard's plots,
which we were very sorry to hear of until we learnt that in the end no
harm came to you. I gather from W. Pekok that my nephew [John II]
knew about it on the Saturday before St Bartholomew, in the king's
household. Nonetheless, Playter and I wrote letters to him, telling him
about the whole business, so that if any questions were asked about it
he should tell the truth, in case the questions were asked by a reputable
man, naming Lord Bourchier, who was with the king at the time.

'I gather from W. Pekok that my nephew is not really very well
known in the king's household, nor with the king's officers. He is not
regarded as being of the household, for the cooks have no order to
serve him and the server has no orders to give him dishes, because the
server will not take dishes to anyone unless he has been instructed by
the controller. Also he knows no one except Wekys; and Wekys had
told him that he would present him to the king; but he has not done so
yet. So it would be best for him to take his leave and come home, until
you have spoken to someone who can help him, for he is not bold
enough to introduce himself.

'But on considering it, I thought that if he came home now the king
would think that when he wanted him for some service somewhere
you had summoned him home, which would mean he would never
get into the king's favour; and also people would think he has been
dismissed from the king's service. And W. Pekok tells me that his
money is spent, not riotously but wisely and discretely, because the expenses in the king's household when the king is on his travels are greater
than you think they are, as William Pekok can tell you. So we must

get a hundred shillings for him, at least, according to William Pekok, and even that will be too little. I know we cannot get even forty pence from Christopher Hansum, so I would be prepared to lend it to him out of my own money. If I was certain that you intended him to come home, I would not send him anything. So I will do what I think would please you best, and that, I think, is to send him the money. So please send me as quickly as you can five marks, and I should be able to get the rest from Christopher Hansum and Luket. Please send it as quickly as you can, because I shall leave myself very short of cash; and please send me a letter saying how you want him to behave.

'Written on Tuesday after St Bartholomew. Christ keep you.'

By Clement Paston

John II's own version of his doings at court was not the same. Writing on August 23, he told his father that he had been busy on his behalf, trying to get a dispute about Dedham manor settled through the lord treasurer, Essex. The king, when asked to favour Paston's case, had replied that 'he will uphold your rights; as for favour, he does not want it to be understood that he should show more favour to one man than another, not to any man in England.' John II continues:

'I am sending Pekok back to you; he is not for me. God send grace that he may do you good service, but I do not think that is likely. You will learn in due course how he behaved here with me. If it did not anger you, I wish you would get rid of him, for he will never do you any good.

'I think that you realise that the money I had from you in London will not last me until the king goes to Wales and comes back again, because I understood that it will be a long time before he comes back. So I have sent to London to my uncle Clement to get a hundred shillings from Christopher Hansum, your servant, and send it to me by my servant, and my armour too, which I left at London to be cleaned. Please do not be angry about this, for I could do nothing else except borrow it from a stranger, one of my companions, which I do not think you would have liked if you had heard of it later. I am confident you will send me another man instead of Pekok.

'My lord of Essex says he will do as much for you as for any esquire in England, and his man Beronners says to me "your father owes much to my lord, because he is a good friend to him", Beronners once suggested to me that you ought to do something for his lord; and I said that I knew you would do whatever you could. He said that you owed a gentleman in Essex called Dorward some money, and that my lord was owed the same amount by the said gentleman, and would like you to settle the amount.

'It is said here that you and Howard had a fight on election day, and that one of Howard's men struck you twice with a dagger; you would have been hurt, it is said, but for a good doublet you had on at the time. Blessed be God that you did have it on.'

In September there were renewed difficulties over the Fastolf properties, this time from Paston's fellow-executors, William Yelverton and William Jenney, who contested the validity of Fastolf's last will, and seized some of Fastolf's manors in Suffolk, in particular that at Cotton. The hall was taken by Yelverton's men and they 'made revel' there, breaking down the bridge and melting the lead on the roof. But efforts by Richard Calle, the Pastons' bailiff, resulted in most of the rents being collected, and although Yelverton managed to get both John Pampyng and Richard Calle arrested on different charges, they were both soon released. Worse was to follow, however: Clement Paston wrote to his brother on October 11:

'*Brother*, I commend myself to you, in due form. I was told by a very reputable man who is a good friend to you, and you to him – you shall know his name in due course, but there is no doubt that he is not the kind of man to tell a lie. On the eleventh day of October the king said, "We have sent two letters under our privy seal to Paston by two yeomen of our chamber; and he disobeys them; but we will send him another tomorrow, and by God's mercy, if he does not come then, he shall die for it. We will make him an example for everyone else to beware of disobeying our writs. A servant of ours has made a complaint against him. I cannot think he has told us the truth about everything, but even so we will not suffer him to disobey our writs; but since he does disobey our writs, we shall be all the more ready to believe that he has behaved as we are told he has done." And at that he made a solemn vow that if you did not come at the third time of commanding, you shall die for it.

'The man who told me this is as learned a man as anyone in England. And also on October 11 he advised me to send a man to you as quickly as possible to let you know about this, and that you should not delay for any reason, but welcome the man and come as quickly as you can to the king, for he is sure that the king will keep his promise.

'So my advice is, if this letter or a messenger reaches you, come to the king and meet him, and when you come, be sure to have a very good excuse. Also, it would be as well to come with a strong escort because Howard's wife was boasting that if any of her husband's men might get at you, your life would not be worth a penny; and Howard has a large company of men here with the king.

'This letter was written on the same day that the king said these words, and the same day that I was told about it, and that was the eleventh of October, as I have said. Tomorrow morning I will send a man to you with this letter, and the same day the king will send the third privy seal to you.

'Also, the man that told me this said it would be better for you to come than to be thrust out of your house by force, and to abide the king's judgement in it, because he will take your obstinacy with great displeasure. I understand that the duke of Norfolk has complained greatly about you to the king, helped by my lord of Suffolk and Howard and Wingfield, who complain to the king about you every day.

'The king is at Greenwich today, and will be there until parliament begins. Some say he will go to Walsingham, but Master Sotill said in the hall at the temple that he had not heard of any such pilgrimage.

'No more for now. Written on October 11 at midnight.

'My nephew John told me that he thought there were proclamations issued against you the same day.'

By Clement Paston your brother

John hastened to London, but his enemies had the upper hand for the moment, and he was imprisoned in the Fleet Prison, probably for about two weeks, leaving Margaret in Norfolk to wait anxiously for news and to do what she could to look after his interest there. On November 2 she wrote:

'*Right worshipful husband*, I commend myself to you. You will be pleased to know that I received the letter you sent by John Holme on last Wednesday. And I received another letter on Friday, at night, which you sent me by Nicholas Newman's man. Thank you for the letters, because otherwise I would have thought that things were going worse with you than they have – or will, by the grace of almighty God. And yet I could not be happy since I had the last letter until today, when the mayor sent a message to say that he had information that he knew was true, and that you had been released from the Fleet and that Howard had been committed to custody because of various serious complaints that were made to the king about him. It was rumoured in Norwich and various other places in the country that you had been committed to the Fleet, and indeed I heard it reported that people were very sorry to hear it, both in Norwich and in the country. You and all who love you should be grateful that you are as popular as you are. You are much indebted to the mayor and to Gilbert, and to various other aldermen, because they do what they can to support you.

'I have spoken to Thomas Howes about the things as you wrote to me about, and he promised that he would do what you wanted as fast as he could; and indeed, as your brother and Playter can tell you, he is, and will be, faithful to you. As for William Worcester, he has been made to feel so anxious, both by the parson and others, as your brother and Playter can tell you, that they think he will do what is wanted. The parson spoke to him very well and plainly. . .

'Please let me know whether you want me to move from here, for it begins to get cold staying here. Thomas Howes and John Russe will finish matters according to your instructions this week, as far as they can, and Howes intends to come to you on the Monday after St Leonard's day. Your brother and Playter should have been with you before now, but they wanted to stay until tomorrow because of the shire court. I spoke to your brother William as you told me to, and he told me, God help him, that he hired two horses two days before you rode away, so that he could ride with you; and because you did not speak to him about riding with you he said he thought you did not want him with you.

'Thomas Fastolf's mother was here the day after you left, wanting to speak to you about her son. She begs you, for reverence of God, to be favourable to him, and help him to gain his rights, so that he can get his estate out of the hands of those who had it during his minority. She says that they are trying to make him a year younger than he is, but she says that he is over 21, and she will take an oath to that effect.

'The blessed Trinity have you in their keeping and send you good fortune in all your affairs, and victory over all your enemies. Written in haste on Sowlmas day.'

By yours, M.P.

Although the quarrel with William seems to have been made up – Agnes Paston was enquiring anxiously about it a fortnight later, according to Margaret – family relations were clearly under stress. In September, James Gloys, who acted as family chaplain, had written to John asking him to make up a quarrel with his mother 'for she is set on great malice, and lets everyone she speaks to know her feelings, and there will be rumours throughout the country until it is quickly stopped'. Reading between the lines – and this can only be a conjecture – the faults were on both sides: John emerges from the letters as a dry, even mean, character, chiefly concerned with business and the winning of a great estate. Against this, he seems to have been law-abiding and loyal to his friends, and genuinely popular in Norwich. At the end of November, Margaret reported:

'The people were never better disposed towards you than they are now. The bill that Howard has drawn up against you and others has put the people in this county in an uproar. God give grace that things do not get any worse than they are.'

John's business at London detained him there throughout the rest of the year, despite Margaret's hope that he might be at home for Christmas: there were problems of communication as well, and Margaret wrote on December 29:

'I could get no messages to London except by sending letters with the sheriff's men; as I knew neither their master nor whether they were friends of yours or not, I thought it was best not to send anything by them.

'And as for the business that John Jenney and James Gresham spoke to me about, I dealt with it as best I could; they both told me that you were sure to be home for Christmas, and that was why I did not send an answer. If I had known that you would not be home by then, I would have sent someone to you, because it seems a long time since I had proper news from you. I am afraid that all is not well with you, since you are away from home at this time of year. Many of your fellow-countrymen think the same, but they are all friendly enough to you, and would be glad to hear news of you.'

But no news came, and ten days later Margaret wrote again, even more urgently:

'*Right worshipful husband*, I commend myself to you. This is to let you know I sent you a letter by Berney's man from Witchingham, which was written on St Thomas's day at Christmas, and I have had no news or letter from you since the week before Christmas, which surprises me very much. I am afraid that all is not well with you, because you have not come home or sent news up to now. I had indeed hoped that you would be home by Twelfth Night at the latest. I beg you with all my heart to be so kind as to send me word how you are as quickly as you can, because my mind will never be easy until I have news from you.

'The people in this part of the world are beginning to grow wild, and it is said here that my lord Clarence and the duke of Suffolk, and certain judges with them, shall come down and try such people as are reputed to be causing riots around here. And it is also said that a new release has been made cancelling what was done at the last shire court. I expect that such talk comes from evil men who want to start a rumour in the country. People here say that they would rather all go up to the king together and complain of the evildoers who have wronged them, than be complained against without good reason and hanged outside their own doors. Indeed, men are very afraid here of a rising of the common people, unless a better way is quickly found of calming the

people, and men are sent down to settle matters whom the people like
and who will be impartial. They do not in the least like the duke of
Suffolk or his mother. They say that all the traitors and extortioners in
this county are maintained by them and by those whose support they
buy in order to maintain the kind of extortion that their underlings
have practised before. Men think that if the duke of Suffolk comes,
things will go badly unless others come with him who are more popular than him. People are much more afraid of being hurt because you
and my cousin Berney have not come home. They say they are sure
that all is not well with you, and if things are not well with you, they
are sure that the men who want to harm you, will soon do them some
harm, and that makes them furious. God in his holy mercy give grace
that a good and sober government is soon set up in these parts, because
I never heard of so much robbery and manslaughter here as there has
been recently.

'As for gathering money, I never saw a worse season, for Richard
Calle says he can get little of the substance of what is owing, either on
your estates or Fastolf's. And John Paston [III] says that those who are
best able to pay, pay worst. They behaved as though they hoped to
have a new world.

'The blessed Trinity have you in their keeping and send us good
news of you. Yelverton is a good friend in hard times for you and
others in these parts, so I am told.

'Written in haste on Thursday after Twelfth Night.'

By your Margaret Paston

This letter evidently produced a reply, since on January 27 Margaret
wrote without asking for news; and she also reported that one source
of difficulty seemed to be removed, because William Worcester had
visited her at Hellesdon at Christmas, and said that he hoped that he
was back in favour with John. Some kind of settlement of his claim
was near, as Thomas Howes reported in February.

'*Right worshipful sir and master*, I commend myself to you. If it so please
you the church at Drayton is or will soon be resigned into the bishop's
hands by John Bullock, and I would be most grateful if you would
agree to my having the presentation at the next vacancy for a nephew

of mine called Reynold Spendelove, and I trust that you will agree to make it in your name and mine, as before. And, sir, I have had various communications with Worcester since Christmas, and I gather from him clearly that he will not agree to any other settlement except his having the lands of Fairchild and other lands in Drayton, worth ten marks in all, direct from you, as well as what he wants from my late master's estate; but I leave this to your noble discretion.

'As for an answer to the notes I have, I have been so sickly since Christmas that I have not yet been able to do it; but I will do it as quickly as I can, and you can use me as an excuse, if you wish, until next law-term, when everything will be answered, by the grace of God, who preserve you and send you the fulfilment of all your desires.

'Sir, if it please you, I was informed very secretly that an army is ready to arrive in these parts of the country, by means of King Henry and the queen that was, and by the duke of Somerset and other, of 120,000 men; and, if the wind and weather had suited them, they should have been here soon after Candlemas. One part should have been on the London side of Trent by Candlemas or soon after, another from Wales and the third from Jersey and Guernsey. So it would be as well to inform my lord Warwick, so that he can speak to the king and good precautions can be taken to withstand their malicious purpose and evil way: God grant we may overcome them, and so we ought, I am sure, if we were all united. There are many meddlers, and those who will do much harm if it comes to the test are highest in favour. God defend us.'

T. Howes

Howes was right that an invasion was afoot, but it did not materialise until later in the year. But there were uneasy stirrings: in February the earl of Oxford and his eldest son were executed for treason. In March John Paston wrote to the sheriff of Norfolk giving the latest information from a captured French ship: only the draft letter survives:

'*Right worshipful sir*, I commend myself to you and let you know that I have been at Sheringham and examined the Frenchmen, sixteen in number, with the master. They say that the duke of Somerset has gone to Scotland, and they say that Lord Hungerford went past Sheringham last Monday in a caravel from Dieppe; there was no great force with him, nor with the duke. They say that the duke of Burgundy has been poisoned and is not likely to recover. And as to forces to be gathered against us, they say that two hundred great ships with forecastles are to come into the Seine from the king of Spain, and three hundred ships from the duke of Brittany, and the French navy; but they have not assembled, and no victuals nor men have been gathered. The king of France has gone on pilgrimage to Spain, with only a few horsemen, they say; for what purpose they cannot tell for sure. In haste at Norwich.'

In May and June both John III and John II were involved in the preparations for repelling any sea-borne invasion. Any royal fleet was usually gathered by 'arresting' merchant vessels for use in war, and John II went to King's Lynn to carry out a warrant for the arrest of a ship called the *Mary Talbot*, about this time: he wrote to his father:

'This is to let you know that I am at Lynn, and gather from various people that the master of Carbrooke wants to take command of the *Mary Talbot* as captain, or so I am told, and to give jackets of his livery to various people who have been hired by other men, and not by him, who are in the ship. For this reason, since I have only a few soldiers in my livery to support me in carrying out the king's commandment, I am keeping your two men Daubeny and Calle with me, and I intend that they shall sail with me to Yarmouth; for I have provided equipment for them, and you will understand that, by the grace of God, the master of Carbrooke will have no command in the ships as I had intended he should, because of his plots. This is one of the particular reasons why I am keeping your men with me, begging you not to be displeased that they are staying here. Despite this, their herding at Wiggenhall shall be done today, by the grace of God, who have you in his keeping.

'Written at Lynn the day after I left you.

'As for news here the messenger will tell you.'

John Paston

John III was less fortunate in his attempts to get a command. His father had tried to get the men of Yarmouth to give him the *Barge of Yarmouth*, but a certain Gilbert Debenham obtained a writ from the king for the command, and he had to give way. John III and Debenham quarrelled publicly about this in London, but apparently their differences were made up by the Paston's old enemy Sir John Howard; and furthermore John II was acting on Howard's behalf over the *Mary Talbot*, so that quarrel appears to have come to an end, possibly after Howard's imprisonment the previous autumn. Equally, the duke of Norfolk had withdrawn from Caister, probably before his death in November 1461 so Paston's position had to some extent improved. Things were peaceful enough in June for him to draw up an inventory of Fastolf's moveable goods;

'A memorandum of the goods that were Sir John Fastolf's, made by John Paston from such examinations and writing as he can find:

'FIRST in gold and silver coin: £2,643 10s.

'ITEM, in silver plate, gilt and ungilt, 13,067 ounces, price gilt 2s 10d, ungilt 2s 6d, amounting to £1615 sterling.

'ITEM, in silver plate, gilt and ungilt, at London, 2525 ounces, and a cup and basin of gold weighing 46 ounces, at 20s the ounce, amounting to £382 20s sterling.

'Sum total of coins and plate valued at £4640 11s 8d.

'ITEM, jewels, brooches and precious stones not valued, 2 cups of gold and 2 ewers weighing 75 ounces.

'ITEM, a flask and two candlesticks of silver weighing 65 ounces lying with the said cups.

'ITEM, jewels pledged by my lord of York to Sir John Fastolf for 600 marks, that is to say: a great diamond in a white rose; a ragged staff with various precious stones given to the king by the assent and commandment of my lord of Canterbury.

'ITEM, a great cross of gold with a flat diamond, a flat ruby and three great pearls.

'ITEM, a little brooch of gold made in the shape of a battlement, with a pointed diamond, a ruby and three pearls.

'ITEM, another brooch made like a falcon, enamelled in white, with a gold buckle.

'ITEM, another brooch made like a trefoil, with an emerald in the middle and a long pearl pendant.

'ITEM, a ring of St Louis with a precious stone in it.

'ITEM, a little gold chain with a pearl pendant and two gold spangles.

'ITEM, a pouch of blue velvet, sealed, with pearls in it.

'ITEM, a gold brooch in the shape of a bushel, with a balasse ruby, a sapphire lozenge, a great orient pearl and a square diamond, lozenged with a gold stripe, garnished with three rubies and three pearls with three gold pendants.

'ITEM, a box of black leather, a brooch of gold in the shape of a wheel with a great sapphire and a great pearl set in it.

'ITEM, a brooch of gold in the shape of an angel, with a flat diamond lozenge-wise adorned with a diamond, a ruby in the middle and two great mother pearls on either side of the angel.

'ITEM, another brooch of gold in the shape of a lady, in it a square cut diamond, a ruby and an emerald in the middle, and two great orient pearls.

'*Arras hangings*

'ITEM, a whole bed or arras of the largest width, ceiler, tester and carving, the pattern a lady sitting in a chair.

'ITEM, eight side-hangings of arras, some large and some small; one is of the siege of Phalist, another of the shepherds and their wives, another of the morris dance, another of Jason and Lancelot, another of a battle, one of the Coronation of Our Lady, another of the Assumption of Our Lady.

'As for an inventory of the wardrobe and bedding and all household stuff remaining at Caister, the said Paston has no certain knowledge or information of it, except of such pieces as he received when he first went to live at Caister, which pieces are specified in a note written on the back of this:

'ITEM, the said John Paston gives the same answer in respect of an inventory of spending money, rings and jewels, silk, linen, woollens and books in French, Latin and English, left in the chamber of the said Fastolf.

'ITEM, likewise, as to an inventory of the wardrobe, bedding and all other household stuff left at Southwark, the said Paston has no certain information about it, and nothing came into his hands except one bed specified on the back of this note.

'ITEM, as for an inventory of live cattle, there were on the manors, an estimated 3000 sheep, valued at 100 marks a thousand, except that certain sheep were taken away by force.

'ITEM, as for horses and all other cattle, the said Paston has no information, except of one ambling horse which had a strained shoulder and was spoilt.

'ITEM, as for an inventory of debts, both by bonds or by account or otherwise due to Sir John Fastolf, the said John Paston has no certain information about them, nor did he receive any part of them.

'This is as much as the said Paston can list at this time about the said inventory without seeing and examining old inventories, memorandums, and bonds of creditors which he does not have in his possession.'

John Paston actually recovered, according to his own records, £1,599 19s 2d of the plate and coin, and household stuff worth forty or fifty marks from Caister, which he carefully listed, down to two old cloths and 'two lavender bags' in the wardrobe and two pewter chargers and a 'brass ladle' in the kitchen. More surprising to us is the list of artillery he acquired, a reminder that Caister was genuinely a fortress equipped for war:

'Two guns with eight chambers shooting a stone seven inches thick, twenty inches compass.

'Two lesser guns with eight chambers shooting a stone five inches thick, fifteen inches compass.

'A serpentine with three chambers shooting a stone of ten inches compass.

'Another serpentine, shooting a stone of seven inches compass.

'Three fowlers shooting a stone of twelve inches compass.

'Two short guns for ships with six chambers.

'Two small serpentines to shoot lead pellets.

'Four guns lying in stocks to shoot lead pellets.

'Seven hand guns with other equipment belonging to the said guns.

'Twenty-four shields of elm board, two of galain [? whalebone].

'Eight old fashioned suits of white armour.

'Ten pairs of body armour, worn out.

'Fourteen horn jackets, worn out.

'Ten bacinets, twenty-four sallets, six gorgets.

'Sixteen lead hammers.

'Nine bills and other pieces of armour and weapons, and zinc caps, and wire of little value.

'Four great crossbows of steel, two of galain, four of yew.

'Two habergeons, and a barrel to store them.'

This private armoury was to come into use in later years in defence of Caister, but for the moment the defence of the kingdom was the main concern. John II accompanied the king on his campaign in the north in the autumn of 1462, when Edward was trying to repel an invasion by a small force of a mere eight hundred men led by Queen Margaret. But this was Percy territory, hostile to the Nevills and to the Yorkists in general, and the great castles of Alnwick, Bamburgh and Dunstan-burgh surrendered to her as soon as she landed. Edward undertook a mid-winter campaign, almost unheard of in medieval warfare, in order to retake them. In mid-November, Margaret herself fled to Scotland, and by the new year, all three castles were back, for the moment, in Edward's hands. Meanwhile, John III had joined the retinue of the young duke of Norfolk and was away on the Welsh border with his master. Like his elder brother, he soon wrote home on November 1, to say that his allowance was insufficient.

'*Right reverend and worshipful father*, I commend myself to you and humbly ask for your blessing. This is to let you know that my lord intends to send for my lady, and is likely to keep his Christmas here in Wales, for the king has asked him to do so. So I ask you to be so kind as to send me some money by the bearer of this, for indeed, as you probably know, I had only two nobles in the purse which Richard Calle brought me by your order when I left you at Norwich. The bearer of this should buy me a gown with part of the money; please give to him enough to buy it with. I have only one gown at Framling-ham and another here, which is my livery gown, and we have to wear a gown almost every day; one gown without a change will soon be worn out.

'As for news, my lord of Warwick advanced into Scotland last Saturday with 20,000 men, and Sir William Tunstall has been captured with the garrison at Bamburgh and is likely to be beheaded, through the actions of Sir Richard Tunstall, his own brother.

'As soon as I hear of any more news I will send it to you, by the grace of God: may he have you in his keeping. Written in haste at the castle of The Holt on Hallowmas day.'

Your son and humble servant J. Paston, junior

A month later, on December 11, he wrote to his brother with the latest news from the northern front, and continued with word of the most recent developments at court.

'The king is at Durham, and my lord of Norfolk at Newcastle; we have enough people here. In case we stay here, please arrange for me to have more money by Christmas Eve at the latest, because I cannot get leave to send any of the men in my pay home again. No one can get leave to go home, unless they leave secretly, and if they were discovered they would be severely punished. Be as cheerful as you can, because there is no danger as yet; if I hear of any threat I will quickly send you word of it, by the grace of God. I am sure you have more news than we have here, but this news is true. Yelverton and Jenney are likely to be heavily punished because they will not come to the king; there are enough complaints against them, and also against John Billingforth and Thomas Playter, which I am sorry about. Please let them know, so that they can send an excuse quickly, so that the king may know why they do not come to him in person. Get them either to come to the king or to let me have their excuse in writing, and I will see that the king knows of their excuse; for I know Lord Hastings and Lord Dacres well, who are now highest in the king's favour; and I also know the younger Mortimer, and Ferrers, Haute, Harper, Cromer and Boswell from the king's household.

'Please let my grandmother and my cousin Clere know that I asked you to let them know the news in this letter, because I promised to send them news. Please let my mother know that I and my companions and servants were in good health when this letter was written, blessed be God. Please let my father know about this letter, and the other letter I sent my mother by Felbrigg's man, and that I beg both him and my mother for their blessing. Please send me a letter to say how you are, and what news you have, because it seems a long time since I had word from you or my mother. Please remember me to my sister Margery and to Mrs Joan Gayne and to everyone at Caister. I have not sent a letter to my father since I left you, because I could not get anyone to go to London since then.

'If you speak to my cousin Margaret Clere, remember me to her, and Almighty God have you in his keeping. Written at Newcastle the Saturday after the Conception of Our Lady.

Yours, John Paston the youngest

'Please let Richard Calle see this letter.'

Early the following year John II was back at home; and his grandmother and others 'made much of him, and were very glad he had come home, and liked his manner very much' according to Margaret. It was a mixed year for him; he was knighted during the year, which was that of his coming of age, but he was also in trouble over allegations that he had committed various crimes in Suffolk. What lay behind this, we do not know, but the trouble blew over. His father was now deep in the lawsuits that threatened over Fastolf's will, and was attempting to collect evidence that would corroborate the validity of the document, getting local people to testify that they had heard Sir John Fastolf declare his intentions long before the actual will was made.

At the end of the year, we have another reminder, as with John II's knighting, that John and Margaret's children were growing up, though the two youngest, Walter and William were only eight and four respectively. On November 13 Margaret wrote to John:

'*Right worshipful husband*, I commend myself to you. This is to let you know that I was at Norwich this week, to get everything that I need for this winter. And I was at my mother's, and while I was there one Wrothe, a kinsman of Elizabeth Clere came in; and he saw your [Margery] and praised her to my mother, and said she was a handsome young woman. My mother asked him to get some good marriage for her if he knew of any. And he said that he knew of a man who would be worth 300 marks a year, son of Sir John Cley who is chamberlain to my lady of York; and he is eighteen. If you think it should be discussed, my mother thinks that it could be arranged for less money as things are now than it will be later – either this match or some other good marriage.

John II – whom we must now call Sir John – ended the year very much out of favour, in contrast to his welcome home in January. Two days after the letter about Margery, Margaret had to write to her eldest son in fairly severe terms:

'I send my greetings, and God's blessing and mine. This is to let you know that I have received a letter from you which you delivered to Master Roger at Lynn, from which I gather that you think you did the wrong thing by leaving without my knowledge. And indeed you did me a bad turn, for your father thought, and still thinks, that I agreed to your leaving and I am very worried about this. I hope that he will take you back into favour if you behave well and do as you should. I charge you on pain of losing my blessing, that you do your duty and work hard to further your father's affairs or anything that would be to the good of his reputation or profit. I am told that you wrote to him in London. What you said I do not know, but although he took little notice of it, I would like you to write to him again as humbly as you can, asking for his favour, and sending him such news as there is from where you are; and you should be careful of your spending, more so than you have been up till now, and live within your means. I am sure that you will find this the best way. I would like you to send me word how you are, and how you have managed since you left here, by some reliable man, and that your father should now know about it. I dare not let him know about the last letter you wrote to me, because he was so angry with me at the time.

'I would like you to speak to Wykes and find out what he feels about Jane Walsham. She has said since he left that unless she can have him she will never be married; her heart is very set on him. She told me that he said to her that there was no woman in the world he loved so well. I would not like him to deceive her, for she is in earnest, and if he will not have her, let me know quickly, and I will arrange something else for her.

'As for your armour and equipment that you left here, it is in

Daubeney's keeping. It was not taken away since you left because he did not have the keys. I think it will deteriorate unless it is attended to in time. Your father does not know where it is. I sent your grey horse to the farrier at Ruston, and he says it will never be fit to ride nor any good for ploughing or carting; he said it is splayed, and the shoulder torn from the body. I do not know what to do with it. Your grandmother would be glad of news from you. It would be as well to send her a letter as quickly as you can.

'God have you in his keeping, and make you a good man, and give you grace to do as well as I want you to do. Written at Caister the Thursday before St Edmund the King.

Your mother, M. Paston

'Please welcome the parson of Filby, the bearer of this, and entertain him if you can.'

Sir John took his time about writing to his father, for the humble letter requested by his mother is dated March 5, 1464, by which time he seems to have been told not to leave home until he had permission to do so. A month later, Margaret, faced by a summons for her husband to join the king, 'with as many persons defensibly arrayed as he might' wrote to John suggesting that Sir John should be sent instead:

'Men here who wish you well think that the least you can do is to send him. As for his behaviour since you left, it has been very good and humble, and he has been diligent in supervising your servants and in other things, which I hope would have pleased you if you had been at home. I hope he will behave well towards you in future. He asked Arblaster to speak to you on his behalf, and very much regretted his behaviour towards you. I sent you word by Arblaster what I did to him after you had gone, and I beg you to take him back into favour, because I hope he is chastised and will be more careful after this. As for other things at home, I hope that I and everyone else will do the best we can; but as for money, that is coming in only slowly.

'God have you in his keeping and send you good speed in all your affairs. Written in haste at Norwich the Sunday after Ascension day. I would be very glad to hear some good news from you.'

By yours, M.P.

Matters over Fastolf's will now came to a head, with the opening in the ecclesiastical courts of the lawsuit against John Paston and Thomas Howes brought by Yelverton and Worcester. This began on April 28, but in February, Clement Paston wrote to John to say that Yelverton had already got judgement in a minor matter:

'*Brother*, I commend myself to you, as usual. As for Hugh Fen's bond, Yelverton acknowledged it probably to be Sir John Fastolf's deed in the exchequer court, and had judgement to receive the money and £10 for damages, and it is reported here that they have a sheriff who will do as they want and grant them execution, or else return that you have wasted the goods under the deed, so they will get execution against your own goods, or a writ to arrest you. So you see that they do not care what they do, even if they should diminish and destroy all the goods under the deed. So in order to save the goods, it would be best to come to some agreement rather than let them all be lost. Also, Yelverton has been to all the tenants at Southwark and ordered them to pay nothing except to him. . .

'Please send 40s that I took to James Gresham and John Pampyng for your business. Also, no one has paid anything in the King's Bench this term for your affairs there, and your clerks and attorney are tired of this. I think I will have to give them something because otherwise they will go unpaid.'

Your brother Clement Paston

On April 18, Clement wrote to say that there were further complications: Thomas Howes seemed to be ill-disposed towards John, for some obscure reason, and the rival party were making moves to found the college, which Sir John Fastolf had provided for in his will, elsewhere. In this, at least, John was successful: after much toil and trouble, he got the necessary licence to found it at Caister in September. But this had meant following the king on his travels, and in the meanwhile his enemies had been busy elsewhere.

A suit had been brought against him by William Jenney in Suffolk for trespass, and after John had failed to appear at four successive sittings, he was declared an outlaw. Although John obtained a writ staying execution in August, writs of outlawry were issued on November

20, though John managed to get another writ of *supersedeas* a week later. He had meanwhile spent a short time in the Fleet prison. To add to his troubles, he had been ill during the summer: in June Margaret wrote to him: 'For God's sake, beware what medicines you take from the London doctors. I shall never trust them because of your father and my uncle, God rest their souls.'

Politically, 1464 had been an eventful year, but the events had taken place in the distant north and in diplomatic negotiations with France. The duke of Somerset's rebellion which began at Christmas 1463, had lasted a brief five months, until his capture and execution at Hexham, and the Yorkists had finally captured the great castles of the north-east by the end of the summer. Abroad, the negotiations with France had apparently resulted in a tripartite alliance between England, Burgundy and France in the summer of 1463, with a clause which stated that the French should in no way help or favour 'Henry, late calling himself king of England'. But the French were anxious to seal this alliance by a marriage between Edward IV and Louis XI's sister-in-law Bona of Savoy; the earl of Warwick, who still wielded great power at court, was equally in favour, but Edward himself scotched these plans by marrying, in secret, the widow of the Lancastrian nobleman Lord Ferrers, Elizabeth Woodville. Although the marriage took place on April 30, the king's council did not learn of it until September 14. Warwick was furious; he had regarded Edward as a figurehead, under his control in the question of marriage and indeed all other matters of policy, and this action was the first of a succession of events which were to disillusion him.

The following year was much quieter in political terms, but quite the reverse for the Pastons. Until now they had managed to hold onto most of Fastolf's lands with relative success, apart from Norfolk's occupation of Caister. But in 1465 they were seriously challenged, not only in the courts, but actually in the manors themselves. John was away in London most of the time, and the business of his estates was in the hands of Margaret, Richard Calle and Daubeney, to whom he sent a long letter on January 15 'about the organisation of my household and estates'; in the covering note to Margaret he also asked for £100 in gold and £20 in silver to be sent, an indication of the expenses of the lawsuit. His letter about the household and estates gives us the best overall picture we have of his business interests and preoccupations:

'Please see that my household and other matters which affect my revenue are well run, and that you, Daubeney and Richard Calle, and such other of my friends and servants as can give you the necessary advice hold a weekly meeting to discuss what needs to be done, or oftener if need be; taking the advice of the master [of the college of priests at Caister], the vicar and James [Gloys] about it, both for the provision of stuff for my household, as well as for the gathering of revenue or corn from my estate, for putting my servants to work, and for the best means of selling and carting my malt and for all other things that need to be done, so that when I come home you do not excuse yourself by saying that you spoke to my servants about it, and Daubeney and Calle do not excuse themselves by saying that they were so busy they could not attend to it. I want my affairs run in such a way that if one man cannot attend to it, another shall be ordered to do it. If my servants fail me, I had rather hire someone for a journey or for a time rather than leave things undone.

'As for my income, I left with Daubeney a note of many of my debts, so that you would all know whether there was money to be collected. I do not like to hear that my priests and alms-people have not been paid and that no money has been sent to me all this time except for ten marks from Berney. All the same, tell Richard Calle that he sent me eight nobles in gold for five marks, and that for as long as gold has been better payment than silver, I never had so much gold from him at once; and tell him that I do not want him to go on doing this, because I think my tenants have little gold with which to pay.

'Remember that in any household, fellowship or company that is well run, arrangements must be made that everyone in it should help and further its prosperity according to his skill and ability, and he who will not do so, unless he is there out of charity, must be expelled from the household or fellowship.

'Since you ask me to pardon your son, I will for your sake take the better course, and want you to know that he will not be so out of favour with me that I will let him suffer harm unless it is his own fault. And although by his presumptions and indiscreet behaviour he caused both me and you displeasure, and set a bad example to my other servants, and although he behaved like that, as everyone knows, because he was weary of staying in my house, and yet could not be sure of help anywhere else, yet all that does not grieve me so much as the fact that I never thought or knew him to be business-like or diligent in looking after himself, but he was always like a drone among bees which work to gather honey in the fields, and the drone does nothing except take a share of it. If this might make him to know better, and remind him that he has wasted his time and lived in idleness, and as a result make him avoid this in future, then it might all turn out for the best. But I have not yet heard from anywhere that he has been that he has behaved or occupied himself; and in the king's household he could not contrive to win the favour or trust of any man of substance who could further his career. Nevertheless, as for your house and mine, I intend that he shall not come there, if I can help it, until he can do more than watch other people and put on a brave face.

'Send me word whether my glazier has finished at Bromholm and at the friars in the south town, and whether he has been paid the money that I sent a message home he should be paid; and if he has done everything he must have more money, but I cannot remember for certain how much until I come home, because I cannot remember what we agreed for the south town. I think Master Clement will know: ask the man himself as well, and send me word. Besides, you and Richard Calle and Daubeney must see that Master Clement and Master Brackley, who are both greatly in need, and my priests and alms-people, are paid, and everyone else as well; and see that I do not have to be called on to pay what I ought to pay. See to it also between you that nothing that is owing to me is lost or passed over by mistake, because that will both hurt and harm my tenants. Remind Richard Calle how the collector at Swansthorpe has got into great debt because no one called on him for just one year, and I think that both John Willeys and the new collector at Snailwell are likely to go the same way, and perhaps Aleyn of Gresham and others.

'Remember that before I ever had anything to do with Fastolf's

estates, when I looked after my own estates, my income was enough
for my expenses both at home and in London and all other costs, and
you put aside money every year in my coffers, as you know. And I
know that the payment of my priests and the other expenses I have in
return for Fastolf's estates are not as great as the income is, even
though part of it is in dispute. And then consider that I have had nothing from my income for my expenses in London for a whole year.
You can easily see that things have not been managed cleverly or discreetly, so I beg you all to put your wits together and see that things
are improved. Think how you would manage if this was yours alone,
and do the same now.

'Remember that I have sent you all many letters about different
things, and also a list of errands lately by Pecock, asking you to look
at them all, and send me an answer item by item; any that you cannot
do now, please do as soon as you can. Read over my letters often until
everything has been done.

'I remember that my hay at Hellesdon last year was used and wasted
in a reckless way, and it was blamed on my sheep. See that it does not
happen again this year.

'Pekok told me of a farmer who wanted Mautby marsh for 12
marks, on the same terms as before; and Richard Calle told me of
someone who would pay more. Burgeys paid me 12 marks 6s 8d at
first, and I had the reed and rushes, and he found the shepherd's wages
also after harvest for my fold; and since then he has whittled away the
shepherd's wages and then the 6s 8d, and I think he is no longer concerned about it. I remember he told me seven years ago that my marsh
would always get worse until the end of the lunar cycle [of nineteen
years], and then it would get better for nine or ten years, promising
that he would then pay the right rent.

'Please let it as well as you can, preferably to him rather than anyone
else if he will match their offer, and confer with Pekok about it.

'. . . As for the matter between Constantine, the parson of Mautby,
and the vicar of Dereham I do not care whether it was important or
not, but I am sure that two witnesses whom I know were interrogated
by an ecclesiastical judge; I think it was Master Robert Popy or someone else. The vicar of Dereham can tell you, and so I think can John

Wynter of Mautby or some other parishioners, where the case between them was held; I think it was in the chapterhouse. If you can safely find out what the witnesses said, that is all I want, but do not go to great expense over it.

'Remember me to Master Robert Popy and tell him that, as far as anything has been said against him over my case, although my adversaries wanted to discredit him, they have only proved him to be a good man, with a good and honest reputation.

'. . . I am told that you have not cut any wood either at Caister or Mautby, which surprises me. Remember that we will need wood to burn in future years.

'I am sending you a list I made while I was at home, of the malt that I estimated I had, reckoning it at the minimum. See that Brigge makes a reckoning of his malt, and add up my list and correct it as necessary; it should not be worse than my total if everyone has done as they should, but I think that few of you will have paid as much attention to it as I did.

'I can sell malt here for 6s 5d a quarter, clean, at Royston measure, which is less than the London water-measure. Cambridgeshire malt is 10s here. Add up what I could sell of new and old, except what I need for my household. Remember that malt from Guton must be shipped at Blakeney. Lynstede's malt at Walcott can be shipped there, so reckon up between you what can best be sold.

'If one man cannot attend to the gathering of money, send another, and send me word of what has been received and spent.

'Let me have an answer to all my letters and to every article in them.

'If you cannot make the necessary arrangements for my priests and alms-people to be paid, besides other charges, and provide money for me as well, either you are collecting badly or else spending foolishly.

'I sent a letter by Ralph Greenacre to James Gresham and to you, which he promised me would reach Norwich on the Wednesday after Twelfth Night. There were various things in it, particularly about a matter that was to be arranged between Yelverton and Robert Wingfield over Caister, as set out in the said letter. It happens that the said Robert will be here within the next two days; if you have found out anything about it, please send me word.

'Young Knyvet tells me that he is my good friend, and he rode home last Friday. Please watch out to see if he interferes in that business and send me word, because I would like to know whether he is true and just, or not; if not, I will not allow him to harm me. Keep a lookout and make inquiries, and find out other people's purposes and keep your own intentions as secret as you can, and whatever boasts are made, be wise and take no notice, but send me word of what you hear.

'Calle sends me word that Thomas Howes is sick and unlikely to recover, and Berney tells me the opposite; so find out about it, and let me know, for although I am not under any obligation to him, I would not want him dead, for more than he is worth.

'Take the vicar the note I am sending you herewith.

'If you can, find some means to discover what Edmund Clere has escheated from anyone.

'Remember to watch your gates by night and day for thieves, for they are riding about different parts of the country with great followings, like lords, and ride from one county into the next.

'Written at London the Tuesday after St Hilary.

'Richard Calle must bring money to me so that my priests can be paid, and he must come safely with other men and attorneys.'

Shortly after this letter, we hear the first reports of a new and serious threat to the Paston estates. The duke of Suffolk, son of William de la Pole, the first duke, who had been executed in such summary fashion in 1450, was now high in the favour of Edward IV: despite his youth, he had fought at the second battle of St Albans, and had officiated at the king's coronation as chief steward of England. Secure in the royal favour, he laid claim to the manors of Drayton and Hellesdon, which lay just across the river from his headquarters in Norfolk at Costessey, by means of spurious deeds and the purchase of dubious titles. But despite these new threats, John would not settle the quarrel with his son, and Margaret was still trying to persuade him to change his mind in April.

'I gather from John Pampyng that you do not want your son taken back into your household or helped by you until the time of year when he was first expelled, that is about St Thomas' mass [end of December].

For God's sake have pity on him and remember that it is a long time since he had anything from you to help him, and he has obeyed you and will do so at all times, and will do all that he can or may to earn your favour. For reverence of God, be a good father to him, and treat him as a father should treat his son. I hope he will know himself better after this and be more careful to avoid things that displease you, and do what pleases you.'

A month later, the situation at Drayton was becoming serious. Suffolk's henchmen seized the horse of one of the tenants while he was ploughing in payment of the rent they claimed, and Margaret had to go down to collect the rents and reassure the tenants, who seemed to be generally favourable to the Paston cause. It seems that the quarrel between father and son was gradually being healed, since she adds:

'Your son will come home tomorrow, I think, and I will let you know how he behaves after this; please do not think I will support or encourage him in any foolishness, for I will not. I will let you know what I think of him.'

A week later, the trouble at Drayton and Hellesdon had escalated. Margaret had retaliated by seizing the plough-team of a tenant who supported Suffolk, 'Piers Warin, otherwise called Piers the sluggard, a flickering fellow,' and Suffolk's men had raided Hellesdon, taking the plough-teams of the parson and another tenant, Thomas Stermyn. The parson was unwilling to do anything about it; he said he would prefer to lose his horses rather than go through with a lawsuit against such men, but Stermyn, after Margaret had interviewed him and stiffened his resolve, agreed to do so under John Paston's guidance. The problem was that although the bishop of Norwich was friendly, the mayor, Thomas Ellis, was definitely hostile:

'I am told that Thomas Ellis of Norwich, who has now been chosen mayor, said at Drayton that if my lord of Suffolk needed a hundred men, he would provide them, and if any men from the town wanted to join Paston he would have them shut up in prison. I would like your men to have a writ of *supersedeas* from the Chancery, and then they would be out of danger from their men here; please do not forget to name Will Naunton in it. Richard Calle and others can tell you how he has behaved, and please do not be angry that he has stayed with me, for he has indeed been a great comfort to me since you left here, as I will tell you later. . .

'I have left John Paston the older at Caister to keep the peace there, as Richard can tell you, for I would prefer, if you agree to be captainess here rather than at Caister. I had only intended to spend a day or two here when I left home, but I will stay here until I hear from you.'

A new family quarrel had also arisen, this time with Agnes Paston, now in her sixties and still a formidable character: Margaret reported at the end of the letter,

'Your mother thinks it very strange that she cannot have the profits of Clere's place peaceably from you. She says it is hers, and she has paid most for it so far, and she says she will either have the profits or make more people talk about it. She says she does not know what right or title you have in it, unless you want to cause trouble; and that would do you no credit. She says she will go there this summer and repair the house there. Indeed, your behaviour to each other is much talked about. I would be very glad, and so would many more of your friends, if things were otherwise between you than they are: if they were different, I think things would go better in your other affairs.

'I pray that God may help all your affairs, and give you grace to bring them quickly to a good settlement, for this is too weary a life to be borne by you and all your people. Written in haste at Hellesdon on May 10. The reason I am sending you this in haste is to get an answer from you quickly.'

Yours M.P.

Ten days later, Margaret reported her latest moves in the battle of nerves over Drayton and Hellesdon. On Saturday, Naunton and Wykis impounded 77 cattle from the tenants of Drayton in lieu of unpaid rent, and drove them to Hellesdon. The tenants appeared soon afterwards, asking for the cattle to be returned, but were told by Margaret that they could only have them if they either paid up or entered into bonds for payments, both of which they refused to do. Meanwhile Suffolk's men threatened the tenants with ejection if they paid, or promised to pay, anything to the Pastons, and one of them went to Margaret offering to return cattle that they had taken in exchange for the release of those seized by her. But she had the upper hand, and refused to let them go until the sheriff finally sent a writ ordering them to be restored to their owners, on the Monday following. On May 27, she wrote to say:

'As for your tenants at Drayton, as far as I can gather, they are very favourable and loyal to you, as far as they can be, and would like you to have the manor back and hold it in peace. They would almost rather be the devil's tenants than the duke's, except for Will Herne, Piers the sluggard, and one Knott of the same town, who are not good men. All your tenants at Hellesdon and Drayton except these three are very glad that we are among them, and so are many other of our friends and neighbours.

'Unless you come home by Wednesday or Thursday in Whitsun week, I intend to see you secretly by Trinity Sunday, unless you send me orders to the contrary before then. . .'

Not all John's supporters were as stout-hearted as his wife. At the beginning of May, John Russe of Yarmouth, who had served Fastolf and was often employed by John, had written to him to say that he thought it was time to settle with his opponents, reminding him that it was a long time since Fastolf's death, and the estates he had left had suffered much from neglect, because Paston was so busy with lawsuits, it would have cost him a quarter of what he had spent on lawyers, and men were saying that he was only continuing out of obstinacy. One case might go well, but there were many others in progress, and each new one meant new costs. 'This law-term they want to see if you will negotiate; if you will not, they will do all they can to defeat you.'

He thought that John suspected anyone who recommended negotiations was in league with his enemies but emphasised that this was not true in his case. He also reported, unlike Margaret, that he 'was sorry to hear that you are not much in favour with gentlemen, and not greatly respected by the common people'. If only he would make his peace, John might be prosperous and in good standing with everyone in Norfolk and Suffolk. It was indeed a 'bold and intimate' letter, and it gives a different view of John, which can only be glimpsed in the letters from his family and confidential servants. Perhaps Russe's portrait may not be too wide of the mark; there are hints of John's miserly, possessive streak elsewhere which would fit well with an obstinate pursuit of his elusive rights under the will.

A new blow fell about the beginning of June, when John seems to have been imprisoned again in the Fleet prison in the course of his lawsuits. This left Margaret virtually in sole charge of affairs: John could advise and admonish from prison, but could do nothing himself. She wrote on June 11:

'*Right worshipful husband,* I commend myself to you. This is to let you know that I received letters from you last Wednesday which were written the Monday before, and I thank you for the letter addressed to me. I want to do the right thing if I can, and if I can, I will do what will please and profit you; in anything beyond my skill, I will take advice from those I know to be your friends, and do as well as I can.

'You wrote to me that Lydham told you that I told him that the duke's men were not so busy as they had been earlier; indeed, they were not at the time, but since then they have been even busier. What support they have I cannot discover as yet, but I think that if all your companions were well-disposed to you, the others would not have as much support as they do have, or else would not be so busy. They make great boasts that the duke will have Drayton, to hold in peace and Hellesdon soon after, all within a short time. They are all the bolder because you are where you are.

'For the reverence of God, if you can manage it by any reasonable or honourable means, get out of there as soon as you can, and come home amongst your friends and tenants, and that would be the greatest comfort they could have, and the contrary for your enemies. . .'

She signs herself 'your faint housewife at this time', as well she might. The following week there were attacks on Costessey; the tenants' cattle and sheep were driven away, and the hall was occupied. The under-sheriff was approached with a view to getting a writ served requiring the return of the castle, but he said that he would not get involved with the men who had done it, even for twenty pounds, and furthermore, the Pastons' enemies were in control of the courts, and in the same week eight of their men were indicted in the local courts, including John Paston III.

John wrote from London on June 27; he clearly had not received the most recent news, and his letter is rather out of touch with what was actually happening, implying that legal means would still win the day for him, and that a word or two from Margaret would offset the campaign of terror by the duke's henchmen. But first there was still the question of John II:

'As for your son, I tell you that I want him to do well, but I cannot see in him any inclination to sense or restraint befitting a man of the world; he merely lives, and always has done, like a dissolute man, making no provision, nor trying to understand the things that a man of property needs to understand. I do not know what he intends to do with himself, except that I think he would like to live again in your house and mine and eat and drink and sleep there. So I tell you that I want to know about him before he knows what I intend, and how well he has occupied his time now he has had leisure. Every poor man that brings up his children to the age of twelve expects then to be helped by his children and to profit by them, and every gentleman of sense expects that his family and servants who live with him and at his expense should help him and further his affairs. As for your son, you know well that he never gave you or me fourpence worth of profit, ease or help, except at Calcott Hall, when he and his brother held it for a day against Debenham; yet it cost me three times as much as Debenham's son ever cost his father. . . So show him no favour until you discover how he is behaving and will behave.'

As to Drayton and Hellesdon, John says that he is going to take the duke to court over this; in his opinion it is all a manoeuvre to distract him from his lawsuit with the duke about Dedham:

'Nevertheless you are a lady, and it is right that you should support your tenants; so I would like you to ride to Hellesdon and Drayton and Sparham, and stay at Drayton, and speak to them. Tell them to stay with their old master until I come, and that you have sent me word recently, but have not yet had an answer. Tell them what I have written, and say openly that it is a shame that anyone should encourage a lord to start such an unjust business, especially a priest; and let them know that as soon as I get home I will see them. . . If any entry is made at Hellesdon, shove them out, and put in someone to keep the house if need be, even though it does not belong to the manor. . .

'[Richard Calle] sent me word that the tenants of Drayton refused to come to the duke's court; if they will be so steadfast to me, and keep their distance from the duke's advisers, the whole thing will be no more than a prank, and will not hurt them; but if they waver it will hurt them.'

At the end of the month, John III went to London to see his father, and his mother wrote to him there about June 30:

'I greet you well; this is to let you know that, as for your sister being with my lady [the duchess of Norfolk], if your father will agree to it I shall be very pleased, because I would rather that she served her than anyone else, so long as she can find favour with my lady. So I would like you to speak to your father about it and let him know that I would be pleased for her to be there if he wants her to go. I would be very glad if she could make her way in the world by marriage or by service, to her advantage, and so that her friends did not need to worry about her; please do what you can, for your own reputation and hers.

'As soon as you can do it without difficulty, please let me have the six marks you know about, because I do not want your father to know about it.

'If you go through London, send me back my chain, and the little chain I lent you before, by some reliable person. If you want my good will, avoid the things I spoke to you about lately in our parish church.

'I pray that God will make you as good a man as any of your family ever were, and may you have God's blessing and mine, and do well.

'Written on the Sunday after you left. Please send news as soon as you can after you reach London how your father and brother are getting on with their business.'

By your mother

An attack on Hellesdon was now clearly impending, and on July 6 Margaret wrote to Sir John, who was now in charge of the house there, warning him to be ready:

'I greet you well; this is to let you know that I am told for certain that the duke of Suffolk is raising a great number of people both in Norfolk and Suffolk to come with him and put us to shame if they can; so I want you to make yourself as strong as you can inside the house, for I and others think that if they do not find you here they will look for you where you are. I want John Paston the younger to ride back to my lady of Norfolk and stay with her until we have more news, as he may be able to do some good there, when he gets any news, by going to his father or to some other place where he might get a remedy. I am told that 200 men have come to Costessey and more than a thousand are on their way. Please send Little John here, as I want to send him on errands for me. Send me word of how you are by some of the tenants who are not well known.'

Two days later, Margaret had joined Sir John at Hellesdon, and they faced their would-be attackers together, as Richard Calle reported to John on July 10:

'Last Monday Master Philip and the bailiff of Costessey, with others of my lord of Suffolk's men were at Hellesdon with three hundred men, intending to have entered, even though they said they had not come to do so. Without doubt, if they had been strong enough for us, they would have entered, and we understood that well enough; but we knew they were coming, and made such preparations for them that we were strong enough. We had 60 men inside the house, and guns and ordnance; so that if they had attacked us they would have been destroyed. And my mistress was in there, and my master Sir John, and has won as great a reputation for that day as any gentleman could have done, and their men say so, and everyone in Norwich.'

Calle goes on to describe how the bishop of Norwich had sent two men to mediate, and how one of Paston's men, Naunton, had gone with Suffolk's men at their request to see the duke. Sir John, on the other hand, told the duke's henchman Harleston that until the duke would be favourable to his father and himself, he had nothing to say to him, and would not go to see him. Calle, like John Russe a little while earlier, urged John to make peace with his enemies, advising him to seek the duke of Norfolk's protection.

'For you must seek some other remedy than what you are doing, or I think things will go to the devil and be destroyed, within a very short time. So, for the reverence of God, make a bargain with Master Yelverton and those who you think will do most damage.

'Please excuse my writing like this, but I am very sorry to see the trouble that my mistress and all your friends have here.'

John had already heard of the goings-on before Calle's letter reached him, and he wrote to Margaret at the end of the week:

'I commend myself to you and thank you for your labour and work with the lawless mob who came to you last Monday, which I heard about from John Hobbes; indeed, you have done well and wisely, and very much to the good of your reputation and mine, and to your adversaries' shame. I am pleased that you proclaimed that Drayton was still in your possession, and would remain so; please make your words good if you can, and at least do not let my adversaries have it in peace if you can.

'John Hobbes tells me that you are not well, which I do not like to hear. Please do not hesitate to take your ease, and in any case do not worry or work too hard over these affairs, and do not take them to heart, and make yourself worse. Unless they overcome you with force or threats, I shall have the manor in more safety than the duke shall have Costessey, never fear. If I do not come home within three weeks, come to me; Wykes has promised to hold the place in your absence. Nonetheless, when you come, make such arrangements as seem best, and safest for both Caister and Hellesdon, if the war continues. If you make peace let me know.'

On August 1, Margaret sent Thomas Bond and James Gloys the parson to hold the manor court at Drayton. She described the consequences of this attempt to enforce the Paston rights in a letter to John on August 7.

'I could get no one else to keep the court there, or to go there, except Thomas Bond, because I think they were frightened of the people who might be there on the duke of Suffolk's side. The said Thomas and James met the duke of Suffolk's men – that is to say Harlesdon, the parson of Sall, Master Philip and William Yelverton, who was steward, with sixty or more people, by estimate – and the tenants of the town, some of them having rusty pole-axes and bills, coming into the manor yard to keep the court. They told them that they had come to keep the court in your name and to proclaim your title. At this the said Harlesdon, without any more words or any occasion given by your men, committed Thomas Bond to the keeping of the new bailiff of Drayton, William Dokket, saying that he should go to the duke and do his errand himself, even though it was James who had delivered the message and spoken; so they took Thomas for no reason. They wanted Thomas to deliver the message and James told them that he had delivered it because he was the more peaceable of the two: after this they told him to get out, and led Thomas Bond off to Costessey, binding his arms behind him with whipcord like a thief. They would have taken him to the duke of Suffolk if I had not spoken to the judges next day before they went to the shire house, telling them of the riots and attacks that had been made on me and my men: the bailiff of Costessey and all the duke of Suffolk's advisers were there, and all the learned men of Norfolk and William Jenney and many people from the county. The judge called the bailiff of Costessey before him and rebuked him soundly, ordering the sheriff to see how many men they had collected at Drayton, and he later came to Hellesdon to see how many people were there, and expressed himself satisfied. Then he rode to Drayton to see who was there, but they had gone before he came; and he asked for Thomas Bond to be handed over to him. They made excuses and said they had sent him to the duke of Suffolk; but afterwards they sent Bond to Norwich to the sheriff, asking that he should not be released without a fine, because he had disturbed the king's court-leet . . ., but when I knew of it I sent Daniel of Marshland and Thomas Bond to tell the judges how the said Thomas had been treated by them, and he did so, and the judges were very [angry] with the duke's men and immediately ordered the sheriff to release Bond without any fine, saying that he ought not to pay one. And indeed I found the judges very gentle and tolerant towards me in my affairs, even though the duke's council had complained to them before I came in the worst possible fashion, accusing us of great assemblies of people and many riotous acts committed by me and your men. I then told the judges that this was untrue, and explained their behaviour and ours, and after the judges learned the truth, they rebuked the bailiff of Costessey severely, in front of me and many others, saying that unless he mended his ways and behaviour they would tell the king and see that he was punished.

'You advised me to get a band of men to keep the court at Drayton with little cost but your council thought it was better not to gather men, because I was told that the duke's men had as many as five hundred men. Your council advised me to get a band of men to keep my house at Hellesdon, for I was told that they were coming to get me out of there, which made me defend it all the more strongly.'

Margaret was now very anxious to see John; the 'three weeks' of his letter of July 13 were already past when she wrote on August 16:

'As for my coming to you, if you want me to come I hope I shall arrange everything before I come so that it shall be safe enough, by the grace of God, until I come back. But for reverence of God, if you can arrange to come home yourself, that would be the best for you; for men cut large thongs out of other men's leather here.'

In the end, it was she who went to London in early September, leaving Sir John and John III in charge of the estates. John III wrote to her in London on September 14:

'After all humble and more dutiful commendation, I beg for your blessing as humbly as I can. This is to let you know that I have written to my father for an answer to the business about which I have written to him urgently; the most important is the manor of Cotton. Please remind him of this, so that I can have an answer as quickly as possible. Also please ask my aunt Poynings to send me an answer about the business she knows of by the same man who brings me an answer about Cotton.

'Also, mother, please arrange by some means that the same messenger shall bring back to me two pairs of hose, one black pair and one brown pair, which are ready for me at the hunchback hosiers' next to Blackfriars Gate in Ludgate. John Pampyng knows him well enough. I think that if the black hose are paid for, he will send me the brown ones without payment. Please do not forget this, because I have not got a whole pair of hose to put on. I think they will cost 8s in all.

'My brother and sister Anne and all the garrison of Hellesdon are well, blessed be God and all ask to be remembered to you. Please visit the Rood at the north door [of St Paul's] and St Saviour's at Bermondsey while you are in London, and take my sister Margery with you to pray to them that she may have a good husband before she comes home again.

'And now please send us some news, as you used to tell me to do. The Holy Trinity have you in keeping, and my fair mistress of the Fleet as well. Written at Norwich on Holy Rood day.'

Your son and humble servant, J. Paston the younger

Margaret left London about September 19: the visit seems to have been a success, as she and John wrote in very affectionate terms to each other after it. John, whose letters are usually practical to a degree, began his next letter with a phrase from the courtly romances of the period:

'*My own dear sovereign lady*, I commend myself to you and thank you for the great welcome you gave me here, to my great cost and charge and labour. But no more of that for the moment, but please send me two ells of worstead to make doublets to wrap me up in this cold winter, and ask where William Paston bought his tippet of fine worstead, which is almost like silk. If it is much finer than what you would buy me for 7s or 8s, buy me a quarter and a sixteenth of a yard to make collars, even if it is dearer than the other; for I want my doublet made all of worstead, in honour of Norfolk, rather than like Gunnor's doublet.'

The letter goes on with the usual list of tasks to be done, accounts to be drawn up, general advice, and complaints about his son's extravagance, ending with a reminder to read the letter over and over again to see that all his instructions were carried out. It ends, however, with a piece of light-hearted doggerel:

'*Item, I shall tell you a tale,*
*Pampying and I have picked your mail**
and taken out pieces five†
If we trust in Calle's promise we may soon unthrive.
And if Calle brings us here twenty pound
You shall have your coins back again, good and round;
or else if he will not pay the value of the pieces there,
To the doorpost nail his ear,
or else do him some other sorrow,
For I want no more for his default to borrow;
Unless the recovery of my income is better plied
He shall by Christ's curse and mine be tried.
See you are cheerful and take no thought,
For this rhyme is cunningly wrought.
My Lord Percy and all this house
Recommend them to you, dog, cat and mouse,
And wish that you had stayed a while
For they say you're a good girl.
No more to you at this time,
But God save him that made this rhyme.

'Written on the eve of St Matthew by your true and trusty husband J.P.'

Margaret's reply a week later also refers to the 'great cheer' she and John had made when they met, saying that John had spent more on entertaining her than she had wanted him to. But with her, too, business takes over almost at once. On her way home, she had seen the sheriff of Suffolk at Sudbury, and had entered the manor at Cotton and stayed there for three days, leaving John III, Wykes and others to gather the rents, and raising support from their neighbours for a planned court day there. In the meanwhile, their adversaries had tried to hold a court at another disputed manor, Calcott, but Daubeney heard of it, and raised sixty men to hold the place. This he did successfully

* bag   † gold coins

despite the appearance of Sir Gilbert Debenham and twenty horse-men. Debenham next appeared at Cotton, to try to prevent John III collecting the rent, as the latter wrote to his father on October 3:

'After all humble and dutiful recommendation, I beg you as humbly as I can for your blessing. This is to let you know that on the Sunday before Michaelmas as my mother came back from London, she came home by way of Cotton; and she sent for me from Hellesdon to join her there, and I have been in the house ever since. As soon as Michael-mas day was past, I began to distrain the tenants and gathered some money (enough to pay for our costs, I think); I am still keeping a good company here and more men were promised, who did not come, and so nearly led to my downfall. When Debenham heard how I had started to collect money, he raised many men within a day and a half, three hundred in all, as I was reliably informed by a yeoman of the chamber of my lord [the duke of Norfolk] who is a friend of mine. This yeoman, as soon as he had seen their company, rode straight to my lord and told him of it; and he also told my lord how I had gathered another great company, exaggerating our number by 150 or more. He said to my lord and lady and to their advisers that unless my lord took charge of the matter there was likely to be great damage on both sides, which would do great harm to my lord's reputation, since he regards us both as his men, and we are well-known as such. When my lord and my lady and their advisers had considered this news and the damage to my lord's reputation if two of his men should fight so close to him, contrary to the king's peace, my lord sent both me and Sir Gilbert Debenham to come to him at Framlingham. Fortunately my mother came to me at Cotton less than half an hour before the mes-senger came to me from my lord, late at night last Tuesday; and the next day I rode to Framlingham to see my lord, and so did Sir Gilbert. As soon as we came, we were summoned to see my lord, and when we came to him he asked both of us to gather our company and to send home again such men as we had got together, and that the court should be put in abeyance until my lord or someone named by him had spoken with both you and Yelverton and Jenney. An impartial man chosen by both of us was to be assigned to keep the peace until both you and they had been spoken to. Then I answered my lord and said that at the time my master was at the manor of Cotton, meaning my mother, and that I could not give an answer until I had spoken to her. So my lord sent Richard Fulmerston, the bearer of this, to my mother today to get an answer. He is to take the answer to my lord in London, for my lord rode to London yesterday; he went all the sooner because he expects to get this matter and everything else between you settled satisfactorily, and thinks that it would be good for his reputation and to his advantage, for then he would expect to have the service of all of you, which would be very valuable to him. The answer that my mother and I gave him was as follows: at the instance of my lord and my lady we would put the court into abeyance and take nothing more of the profits of the manor until she and I heard again from my lord and you, provided that the others would neither make entry nor distrain the tenants nor keep court any more than we would; and we told Richard Fulmerston that my mother and I did this at the instance and urgent request of my lord, because my lord wanted to make peace, and we would not oppose a reasonable settlement; but we said that you would not thank us for doing so unless you knew that it was at my lord's request. But before we made this answer we had received almost as much money as Richard Calle's books indicated we should collect; and as for possession of the place, we told him we would keep it, and Sir Gilbert agreed, provided Yelverton and Jenney did likewise. It was time for him to say so, because my lord told him he would have chained him by the feet otherwise, to make sure that he made no disturbances before my lord came back from London. I think, and my mother does too, that this agreement was made at a good moment, because I was let down by 150 men who had been promised to come to me when I sent for them. . .'

John III's shrewd handling of the affair, in contrast to his elder brother's fecklessness, foreshadows the later fortunes of the family; but his triumph was only a temporary respite for, on October 14, the long-feared attack on Hellesdon materialised. We have no description of the attack itself, but it seems that Sir John and his sister Margery were in the house, and were seized and taken out: the duke's men then ransacked the place and spent the next three days pulling down all the buildings. It was a dangerous time for the Pastons and their supporters as Margaret describes in a letter written three days after the attack:

'On Tuesday morning John Botillere, also John Palmer, Darcy Arnald your cook and William Malthouse of Aylsham were seized at Hellesdon by the bailiff of Eye, called Bottisforth, and taken to Costessey, and they are being kept there still without any warrant or authority from a justice of the peace; and they say they will carry them off to Eye prison and as many others of your men and tenants as they can get who are friendly towards you or have supported you, and they threaten to kill or imprison them.

'The duke came to Norwich at 10 o'clock on Tuesday with five hundred men and he sent for the mayor, aldermen and sheriffs, asking them in the king's name that they should enquire of the constables of every ward within the city which men had been on your side or had helped or supported your men at the time of any of these gatherings and if they could find any they should take them and arrest them and punish them; which the mayor did, and will do anything he can for him and his men. At this the mayor has arrested a man who was with me, called Robert Lovegold, a brazier, and threatened him that he shall be hanged by the neck. So I would be glad if you could get a writ sent down for his release, if you think it can be done. He was only with me when Harlesdon and others attacked me at Lammas. He is very true and faithful to you, so I would like him to be helped. I have no one attending me who dares to be known, except Little John. William Naunton is here with me, but he dares not be known because he is much threatened. I am told that the old lady and the duke have been frequently set against us by what Harlesdon, the bailiff of Costessey, Andrews and Doget the bailiff's son and other false villains have told them, who want this affair pursued for their own pleasure; there are evil rumours about it in this part of the world and other places.

'As for Sir John Heveningham, Sir John Wyndefeld and other respectable men, they have been made into their catspaws, which will not do their reputation any good after this, I think. I spoke to Sir John Heveningham and told him the truth of the matter, and how we had behaved at Drayton, and he said that he wished everything was settled and that he would tell my lord what I had said; but Harlesdon was the only one he listened to, and the duke only acted on his and Dr Aleyn's advice.

'The lodge and remainder of your place was demolished on Tuesday and Wednesday, and the duke rode on Wednesday to Drayton and then to Costessey while the lodge at Hellesdon was being demolished. Last night at midnight Thomas Slyford, Green, Porter and John Botesforth the bailiff of Eye and others got a cart and took away the featherbeds and all the stuff of ours that was left at the parson's and Thomas Water's house for safe-keeping. I will send you lists later, as accurately as I can, of the things we have lost. Please let me know what you want me to do, whether you want me to stay at Caister or come to you in London.

'I have no time to write any more. God have you in his keeping. Written at Norwich on St Luke's eve.'

M.P.

Ten days later, she wrote with fuller details of the damage that had been done, and of the local reaction to it.

'I was at Hellesdon last Thursday and saw the place there, and indeed no one can imagine what a horrible mess it is unless they see it. Many people come out each day, both from Norwich and elsewhere, to look at it, and they talk of it as a great shame. The duke would have done better to lose £1000 than to have caused this to be done, and you have all the more goodwill from people because it has been done so foully. And they made your tenants at Hellesdon and Drayton, and others, help them to break down the walls of both the house and the lodge: God knows, it was against their will, but they did not dare do otherwise for fear. I have spoken with your tenants both at Hellesdon and Drayton, and encouraged them as best I can.

'The duke's men ransacked the church, and carried off all the goods that were left there, both ours and the tenants, and left little behind; they stood on the high altar and ransacked the images, and took away everything they could find. They shut the parson out of the church until they had finished, and ransacked everyone's house in the town

five or six times. The ringleaders in the thefts were the bailiff of Eye
and the bailiff of Stradbroke, Thomas Slyford. And Slyford was the
leader in robbing the church and, after the bailiff of Eye, it is he who
has most of the proceeds of the robbery. As for the lead, brass, pewter,
iron, doors, gates, and other household stuff, men from Costessey and
Cawston have got it, and what they could not carry they hacked up in
the most spiteful fashion. If possible, I would like some reputable men
to be sent for from the king, to see how things are both there and at the
lodge, before any snows come, so that they can report the truth, because otherwise it will not be so plain as it is now. For reverence of
God, finish your business now, for the expense and trouble we have
each day is horrible, and it will be like this until you have finished; and
your men dare not go around collecting your rents, while we keep
here every day more than twenty people to save ourselves and the
place; for indeed, if the place had not been strongly defended, the duke
would have come here.

'The mayor of Norwich arrested the bailiff of Normandy's, Lovegold, Gregory Cordoner and Bartholomew Fuller without any authority, except that he says he has an order of the duke's to do so; and
he would not let them out of prison until he had security of £80 for
each of them to answer to such matters as the duke and his council
want to accuse them of, at any time that they are summoned; and he
will do the same to any others he can catch who are well disposed towards you. The mayor also wanted them to swear that they would
never oppose the duke or any of his men, which they refused to do.
Poor Bartholomew is still in prison for lack of security. He used to be
a great supporter of good old Edmund Clere. Arblaster thinks that
Hugh at Fen could do much for you, and he thinks he would be reliable, if you agree to it.

'For the reverence of God, if any respectable and profitable method
can be used to settle your business, do not neglect it, so that we can get
out of these troubles and the great costs and expenses we have and may
have in future. It is thought here that if my lord of Norfolk would act
on your behalf, and got a commission to enquire into the riots and rob-
beries committed on you and others in this part of the world, then the
whole county will wait on him and do as you wish, for people love

and respect him more than any other lord, except the king and my lord of Warwick. . .

'Please do let me know quickly how you are and how your affairs are going, and let me know how your sons are. I came home late last night, and will be here until I hear from you again. Wykes came home on Saturday, but he did not meet your sons.

'God have you in his keeping and send us good news from you. Written in haste on the eve of St Simon and St Jude.'

By yours, M.P.

About the same time, Margaret drew up a long list of the household stuff stolen or destroyed at Hellesdon, ranging from large quantities of bedding, linen and kitchen equipment to arms and armour from the church, and personal possessions; these included gold thread belonging to Margery Paston, as well as an ivory hand mirror and a comb of hers, a diamond ring belonging to Joan Gayne, and armour and 'a book of French' belonging to Sir John Paston.

As if these troubles were not enough, early in 1466 a new enemy appeared. Reviving old rumours about the origins of the Pastons, Lord Scales persuaded the mayor and city officers in Norwich to seize John's property there on the grounds that he was in fact legally a serf on lands belonging to Lord Scales. The case was settled later in the year, when Sir John and his brothers produced abundant evidence that this was not the case. The genealogy they offered, like so many medieval descents, began with a spurious ancestor, one 'Wulfstan, who came out of France' – an unlikely provenance for a man with an Anglo-Saxon name!

But John was still unable to bring the major law-suits to a close; and few letters for this period survive, apart from a note about legal technicalities from his brother Clement in March, which ends with a familiar plea for more money for his nephew Sir John, who is about to go to Scotland with the king, and whose 'great horse is likely to die'. We have another glimpse of Sir John and his preoccupations in a letter to him from John Wykes in February:

'*Right worshipful and my especial good master*, I commend myself to you, and let you know that the bearer of this told me that you were very surprised that I had not sent you word nor any letter in answer to the letters that you sent me in London. You sent me one letter by Richard, Playter's man, and I sent you an answer to it by a man of the prior of Bromholm's; as for other letters, none came to me except that one.

'Master Fleming enquires every day about his horse, and every time I meet him he asks me when his horse will come, and when I will hear from you. Please send me word in a letter as to how I should answer him, and if the horse is to be sent, let me know when; for if he had not been sure of its return, he would have hired it out elsewhere.

'John Otter is not yet paid, but I expect it will not be long before he gets his money, because he has spoken again to my master your father about it; as for Gilmin, he has not spoken to my master as yet.

'I think your father will be favourable to you, for John Say talked to him frankly about his behaviour towards you, and told him that he was less popular because of the way he treated you.

'The earl of Arundel's son has married the queen's sister.

'Lord Lovel's son has married Lady Fitzhugh's sister.

'Jenney wants to settle with my master, and spoke to my master about it himself in Westminster Hall.

'Everyone in the king's household is well, and wish that you were there.

'No more at the moment, but the Holy Trinity have you in keeping. Written at London the Monday after St Valentine.'

Your servant, John Wykes

Sir John's carefree days as a young courtier were soon to be over. Although his father seems to have come almost to the end of the lawsuit over Fastolf's will, the strain of this and the troubles in Norfolk had been very great. On May 21, John died in London. We know nothing of the circumstances surrounding his death, and the date only appears in the legal documents settling his estate, rather than in any letters. There is no surviving will, (though one was certainly made), which might indicate that his death was sudden and unexpected, but again the absence of correspondence – there are only four letters written by members of the family for the whole of 1466 – means that we can only guess. At all events, Sir John took over the administration of the estates, under his mother's watchful eye, and in July was able to get a warrant from the king which restored to him most of the lands held by his father, and much of the Fastolf estate as well. This warrant was a settlement of the dispute with Lord Scales, but it also boded well for the future. About the same time, he gained the patronage of John de Vere, earl of Oxford, which was to stand him in good stead in future years. On July 31, the earl wrote to him to warn him of an impending attack on his rights at Cotton, by Sir Gilbert Debenham and Sir John Howard. At the end of October, his mother wrote to him with advice about his father's will:

'I greet you well, and send you God's blessing and mine. Please send me word how your business is going, for it seems a long time since I had news from you. I advise you at all costs to keep carefully your documents that are important, so that they do not fall into the hands of people who could use them to your harm. Your father, God have mercy on his soul, valued his documents more, when he was in trouble, than he did any of his moveable goods. Remember that if they were taken from you, you could never get any more like them.

'I would like you to watch out and see if any proceedings are taken against me or against any of those who were indicted before the coroner, so that I know about it and can take steps to remedy it.

'As for your father's will, please take good advice about it, for I am told that probate can be granted, even though no one takes responsibility this year. You can get a letter of administration for whoever you want, and administer the goods, and not take the responsibility. I advise you not to take responsibility until you know more than you do as yet, because you can be sure, from what your uncle Will said to you and me that they will make you and me responsible for more things than are laid down in your father's will, which would be too great an expense for either of us to bear. As for me, I will not be in a hurry to take responsibility, I assure you.

'For the reverence of God, manage your affairs this law-term so that we can rest after this, and do not cease to work at it for the time being; and remember how much all this has cost up till now, and reflect that it cannot go on much longer. You know how much you left when you were last at home, and I can tell you that there is no more in this part of the world with which to pay any expenses. I advise you to enquire discreetly if any more can be got where you are, for otherwise I think things will not go well with us. Send me word quickly how you are, and whether you have got the deeds which were missing last time, because they are obviously not down here. I am told confidentially that Richard Calle has almost won over your uncle Will with good promises about his estates and other things which would be much to his advantage, so he says. Beware of him and his fellows, by my advice.

'God send you good speed in all your affairs. Written at Caister the day after St Simon and Jude; I would not be here but for your sake.'

By your mother

Early the following year, the letters reflect a new pattern; instead of John busy at the law-courts, worrying about money and the management of his estates, we have Sir John at court, borrowing money where he can and leaving the day-to-day work in the hands of his younger brother. On January 29, Thomas Daverse, a fellow-courtier, wrote to him:

'. . . I gather from you that money might enable you to settle your affairs this term; if you can be in London on Monday night or Tuesday before noon I think that I have found a means to get £100 or 200 marks lent to you on security for half a year without any formal arrangement or loss of goods by you; William Rabbes can tell you more.

'As for Ovid's *De Arte Amandi* I will send it to you next week, for I have not finished with it yet. But I think Ovid's *De Remedio* would be more suitable for you, unless you intend to fall into the lap – as white as whalebone – of Lady Anne P. within a very short time. You are the best chooser of a lady that I know.

'Please remember me to my lord of Oxford and to my good masters, Needham, Richmond, Chippenham, Staveley, Bloxham, Stuart and Ingleton especially, and all my other good masters and friends generally. And Mrs Gaydade asks to be remembered to you and said, that if you are feeling generous she would like a new ribbon for her hair.

'Written at London on January 24.'

With heart and service, your T.D.

Despite Sir John's pursuit of his pleasures, he could not avoid being involved in the inquiry into Fastolf's will which began during the spring. William, his uncle, was at this point active in helping him against Yelverton, who remained his principal opponent in the courts, and he, Margaret and Sir John spent most of the early part of 1467 in London. Each side was busy marshalling its witnesses, and doing its best to discredit those produced by the other side. John III describes some of the manoeuvres that were going on in a letter on February 7 to Sir John:

'*Sir*, this Saturday John Russe sent me word by Robert Botler that William Yelverton has been in Yarmouth for the last three days to get new witnesses to go up to London. John Russe and Robert Botler think that they are to give witness to prove that Sir John Fastolf's will was that 400 marks a year should be amortised to the college, and also that the estates that my father took here at Caister at Lammas before Sir John Fastolf died were delivered to my father with the intention that he should use them to carry out the will. Bartholomew Elys, John Appylby and John Clerk are the witnesses. As for Bartholomew Elys, he is outlawed, and people say in Yarmouth that he is encouraging a cleric of Yarmouth and his own wife to have an affair. As for John Appylby, he is half-mad, and taken for such in the town, even though he is an attorney, as Bartholomew Elys is, in the bailiff's court at Yarmouth. As for John Clerk of Gorleston, he was outlawed in a case brought by Sir John Fastolf and various others. . .'

Important additional evidence came to hand in that month in connection with Friar Brackley, who had been one of Fastolf's intimates. He had told his confessor, John Mowth, two or three days before his death, that the will was indeed Fastolf's; then he recovered, but relapsed, and just before his death said to him 'Sir, since you asked me of your own accord to say on my conscience what I know about Sir John Fastolf's will, now of my own accord and to unburden my soul, because I know I cannot recover but will soon die, I ask you to report after my death that I took it on my soul on my deathbed that the will that John Paston put in for probate was Sir John Fastolf's will.'

In April, Richard Calle was busy organising witnesses on the

Pastons' behalf. At last on August 7, the first victory was won, probate being granted to Sir John and Thomas Howes. Though there was a long way to go before the matter was settled, this was an important step forward.

Sir John, meanwhile, continued to lead a courtier's life, but he also did what he could to advance the family's interest. Possibilities of marriage were in the air: during the year there was an offer for Margery's hand, of £40 settlement and two hundred marks a year inheritance, from a certain John Strange on his nephew's behalf; but the matter went no further. Sir John had grander ideas, perhaps; certainly he was looking for a bride from among the nobility for his brother, and wrote in March:

'*Right worshipful and truly well-beloved brother*, I recommend myself to you with all my heart, and thank you for your hard work and diligence in keeping my place at Caister so securely with all your energy, which has kept you fully occupied; in return, I have had so little leisure that I have only done a few of your errands and could not do more until now.

'As for Lady Boleyn's feelings towards you, I cannot get her to agree on any terms that you should have her daughter [Alice] for all the private means that I employed; indeed, she gave me so little encouragement, that I was reluctant to speak to her myself about it. However, I gather that she says: "If he and she can agree, I will not stop them; but I will never advise her to have him." Last Tuesday she rode back to Norfolk; so if you think you can find a way to speak to her yourself, do so, for in my opinion it will never come about unless you do. As for Crosseby, I gather that no marriage has been settled between them, though there is much talk of it.

'You are presentable, and perhaps once the girl has seen you, and you have told her that you like her, telling her to keep it secret, you may be able to find a way, with her help, to bring this about, which will please both you and her; but you cannot do it without some encouragement from her. Be as humble as you can towards her mother but not too humble towards the girl, and do not seem too anxious to succeed or too sorry to fail. I will always act as your herald, both here, if she comes here, and at home when I come home, which I hope will be soon, and within forty days at the most. My mother has a letter which can tell you more, and you can let Daubeney see it.

John Paston, K

'If you ask R. Calle properly, he will let you have some money. I have written to him often enough.'

Shortly afterwards, Sir John took part in a tournament at Eltham, the king's favourite palace, where Edward was in the process of building a magnificent new great hall. His letter about it only survives in part:

'My hand was hurt at the tourney at Eltham on Wednesday last. I wish you had been there and seen it, for it was the best sight that has been seen in England for the last forty years with so few taking part. There were on one side within [? as defenders], the king, Lord Scales, myself and Sellinger, and without, my Lord Chamberlain, Sir John Woodville, Sir Thomas Montgomery and John Parr.'

John III's response was:

'. . . you said that you wished I had been at Eltham to see the good sight of the tourney there; I had much rather see you once in Caister Hall than see as many king's tourneys between Eltham and London as you like.

'You wanted to know what I had done about Lady Boleyn. Indeed, I have neither spoken to her nor done anything about it, nor will I do anything until you come home, even if you do not come for seven years. Nonetheless, Lady Boleyn was in Norwich the week after Easter, from the Saturday till the Wednesday, and Heydon's wife and Mistress Alice as well; and I was at Caister and did not know of it. Her men said that she had no business to do in the town but was there for her pleasure; but I think that she expected me to go to Norwich to see her daughter.

'I beg you with all my heart, come home, even if you only stay for a day; for I promise you that your people think you have forgotten them. Most of them must leave at Whitsuntide, because they cannot stay any longer.

Your J. Paston

'As for R. Calle, we cannot get an eighth of the money we pay out for the household alone, quite apart from men's wages. Daubeny and I can do nothing more without ready money.'

John III's report had little effect. On May 1, Sir John was cheerfully laying bets with a fellow-courtier about affairs of state:

'This note of indenture made the first of May in the seventh year of the reign of King Edward the Fourth between John Paston, knight, of the one party and Thomas Lomnour of London, mercer, on the other party, witnesses that the said Thomas Lomnour has bargained, covenanted and agreed with the said John Paston in the form following, that is to say, that the same Thomas has sold to the said John an ambling horse, upon this condition: if the day of marriage between the Lord Charles, son and heir to the duke of Burgundy, and my lady Margaret, sister to our sovereign lord the king aforesaid, takes effect, and the same Lady Margaret is lawfully married to the said Lord Charles within two years from the date of this present note, then on the date of the same marriage the said John Paston agrees to pay to the said Thomas Lomnour for the said horse 6 marks (80s). If the said marriage does not take effect within the said two years, the said John Paston agrees to pay to the said Thomas Lomnour after the two year period aforesaid forty shillings and no more.'

Sir John failed to get his horse at half-price, because, as we shall see, the marriage took place in 1468. Meanwhile, there were new threats to his estates; a favourite of the queen's, Simon Blyaunt, was claiming the manor of Cotton, but thanks to the staunch support of the earl of Oxford, this threat was repulsed. It does appear, however, that Sir John had to give the earl an interest in the manor revenues in return. In July, his mother sent him warning of renewed difficulties at Caister and Hellesdon:

' I greet you well and send you God's blessing and mine. This is to let you know that Blickling of Hellesdon came from London this week; he is very cheerful and boasts that within a fortnight there will be new lords and officers at Hellesdon. Today I was brought word from Caister that Rising of Fritton heard in various places when he was in

Suffolk that Fastolf of Cowhaugh is gathering all the men he can and intends to attack Caister and enter it if he can; it is said that he has a hundred men ready and sends spies every day to discover how many men are keeping the place. I do not know by whose power, favour or support he will do this, but you know that I have been attacked there before now, when I had more encouragement than I have now. I cannot control or take charge of soldiers well, and they do not esteem a woman as they would a man. So I would like you to send home your brother or Daubeney to take charge and to take in as many men as are necessary to safeguard the place. If I was there without responsible or respectable people with me, and a rabble of knaves came and succeeded in doing what they wanted, it would be a disgrace to me.

'I have been going round my estates to put things in order, as I wrote to you; matters are not settled to my liking, and I did not want to go to Caister until it was done. I do not want to spend any more time there unless I have to; so at all events send someone home to keep the place. When I have done and settled everything I have started, I will go that way if I can do any good there. I have sent a message to Nicholas and those who keep the place that they should take in some fellows to assist and strengthen them, until you send different instructions or some other man home to govern the garrison. I am very surprised that you have sent me no word as to how you are; for your enemies are getting very bold and that makes your friends both fearful and doubtful. So please hearten them, so that they cease to be discouraged; for if we lose our friends it will be hard, in this troubled world, to get them again.'

The problems over money persisted, and at the end of the year Sir John was contemplating the sale or mortgage of some of his estates, to the disgust of his mother and brother. John III wrote to his mother in the autumn:

'*Right worshipful mother*, I commend myself to you, humbly begging for your blessing. This is to let you know that my brother and I are in good health, blessed be God, and all our company; and as for me, I trust to God to see you by Hallowmas [November 1] or within four days after that at the latest, at which time I hope to find means to relieve you of such people of my brother's as you are keeping with you. I shall have to do it from my own resources, for my brother is incapable of doing it; I assure you, so God help me, he has at the moment not a penny in his purse, and does not know where to get any.

'As for Beckham, I warrant that if you will send the plate which you and I are in charge of to help pay his debts and to sue out his judgement this law-term, it shall be neither mortgaged nor sold. So mother, both he and I beg you to send him the plate by Juddy, or else, God help me, I do not know what will happen to him; by the faith I owe to God, he expects to be arrested any day, and I think he will be. Juddy will need to be sent quickly, lest such an arrest happens in the meanwhile.

'As for my lord of Norfolk, I am promised his favour, but I must wait a while, as my lady told you, for the sake of appearances.

'As for news, God help us, neither the king nor the lords can agree for certain whether they shall go together once more to the war or not. When I hear for certain, I will let you know. You can send money by Juddy for my sister Anne's hood and for the sarsenet tippet, 8s a yard for damask and 5s for sarsenet; her hood will take three-quarters of a yard.

'No more, for lack of leisure; but I pray God send you his heart's desire, and other poor fools theirs.'

Your son and humble servant J. Paston

The disagreements between Edward and his lords which John III so briefly reports were of increasing importance. Ever since Edward's secret marriage to Elizabeth Woodville, Warwick had been discontented with the king, whom he regarded as his protégé, a puppet who would occupy the throne while he held real power. Unfortunately he had misjudged his man, and Edward's marriage was the culmination of a series of actions which made plain that the king was indeed his own master. Warwick was still anxious to secure an alliance with France, but instead Edward negotiated a treaty with France's arch-enemy Burgundy, partly as a deliberate rebuff to Warwick. Equally, just as the Neville family had once dominated the political scene, it was now the turn of the Woodvilles.

In June 1467 Warwick's brother George, archbishop of York, was dismissed from the chancellorship. For the moment, there was no public breach between Edward and Warwick, but the air was full of intrigues.

In April, plans for the marriage of Charles of Burgundy and Princess Margaret were settled, and a royal writ was sent to Sir John requesting him to accompany the bride to Flanders. Among the other members of the retinue were Lord Scales, once an adversary of the Pastons but now apparently on friendly terms with Sir John, and the duchess of Norfolk. John III also went, and on July 8 he wrote from Bruges to his mother:

'As for news here, all that I can send you is about the festival, except that my lady Margaret was married last Sunday at a town called Damme, three miles outside Bruges, at five o'clock in the morning and she was brought the same day to Bruges to dine, and was received there with as much honour as everyone could devise, with a procession of lords and ladies better arrayed than anyone I ever saw or heard of; and many pageants were played along her route to Bruges, the best that I ever saw. And the same Sunday my lord the Bastard undertook to hold the lists against 24 knights and gentlemen within eight days in jousts of peace; and when they had jousted, those 24 and he himself would tourney against another 25 the following day, which is next Monday. And those who jousted with him up to today have been as richly equipped – and he himself as well – as cloth of gold and silk and silver- and gold-smiths' work could make them; for those of the duke's court, both gentlemen and ladies, have no lack of such stuff, nor of gold, pearls and jewels. Unless someone got it by just wishing, I have never heard of such plenty as there is here.

'Today Lord Scales jousted with a lord from this country, but not with the Bastard, for they promised each other at London that neither of them would ever bear arms against each other. But the Bastard was one of the lords who brought Lord Scales into the lists, and by accident a horse kicked my lord Bastard on the leg and hurt him so badly that I am afraid he will be unable to accomplish his feat of arms, which is a great pity, as indeed I think that God never made a more honourable knight.

'As for the duke's court, I never heard of one like it for lords, ladies and gentlemen, knights, squires and gentlemen, except for King Arthur's court. Indeed, I have not the wit or memory to write to you of half the noble events here; but what I have left out, I will tell you when I remember it when I come home, which I trust to God will not be very long. For we depart from Bruges for home on Tuesday next, as well as everyone else who came from England with my lady of Burgundy; except for those who are staying in her company, which I think are only a few. We are leaving all the sooner because the duke has heard that the French king intends to make war on him very soon, and that he is within four or five days' journey of Bruges; and the duke is riding to meet him on Tuesday next. God send him good fortune, and all his men, for indeed they are the finest company I ever came across, and can behave better than anyone else, in the most gentlemanly fashion.

'We have no other news here, except that the duke of Somerset and all his men left Bruges in good order the day before my lady the duchess came here; and they say here that he has gone to ex-Queen Margaret, and will not be helped again by the duke.'

During the course of 1468, there were two important developments in the dispute over Fastolf's will: William Worcester was reconciled with the family, but Thomas Howes, named as John Paston's co-executor in the last will, now denied that this was genuinely the old man's last testament, and provided an account of how Paston had forged it. William Worcester wrote to Margaret Paston at some time during the year, giving his version of the quarrel between him and her husband with news of new developments since the executors under the earlier wills signed a document releasing Caister to Sir John, following the probate of August 1467.

'*Right worshipful mistress*, after due commendations, you will be glad to know that I spoke lately with your son Sir John Paston about the foundation of my master Fastolf's college at Cambridge, if it is not founded at either Caister or St Benet's, because that university is near the counties of Norfolk and Suffolk. Although the bishop of Winchester is disposed to found a college in Oxford where my master shall be prayed for, he could make some other memorial in Cambridge with much less expense, perhaps of two clerks and three or four scholars, founded with the value of good benefices and rich parsonages, whose advowsons could be purchased for far less than lordships of manors can. I found your son favourable to the idea, and he will put it to my lord bishop.

'Besides, in Christmas week, before the feast at London, my lord bishop of Winchester called me to him in the presence of Sir John and asked him to be favourable to me, and my master would not let me say anything; and he spoke very well. Would to Jesu, mistress, that my good master who used to be your husband, could have found it in his heart to have trusted and loved me as my Master Fastolf, and as he himself showed that he could when Fastolf was alive. Then he would not have believed the malicious invented tales that Friar Brackley, W. Barker and others falsely made up about me, with all due respect. And now you can know the truth, and your son Sir John as well. And yet for all that I never put my master Fastolf's estates in trouble, for all the unkindness and greed that was shown towards me.

'I am very glad that Caister is and shall be at your command, yours especially. It is a rich jewel for the whole country when needed, in time of war; and my master Fastolf would never have built it if it was going to come under the control of any sovereign who would oppress the country. I find that the monks of St Benet's have unkindly taken away a room which the old abbot gave me possession of for my solace when I went there to relax, and gave the room to Master John Smyth, who so Thomas Howes told me, was a far from honest adviser about the revision of the last will, which gave two executors alone control. I wish he had never meddled with it; that advice made much trouble. . .

'And, mistress, may I be so bold as to ask you to remember me to my best mistress, your mother Agnes, for she favoured me and was very charitable towards me, to make me better disposed towards her son Master John; and on my soul, it made me all the keener to save the estates from trouble or claims. I declare before the whole world that I never caused trouble on any manor or estates of my master Fastolf's, nor gave anyone the title deeds to a place; and you can talk to her about it when you are alone.'

Thomas Howes, on the other hand, was a dangerous man to have as an enemy, because he held joint powers as executor even under the will by which the Pastons inherited. In the autumn of 1468, he appeared openly in the opposite camp, issuing a formal statement denying the validity of the will made on Fastolf's deathbed, and describing it as forged by John Paston:

'On Monday November 5, the day that Fastolf died at about six p.m., the said Sir Thomas Howes at about three o'clock came into the lower hall at Caister. He saw John Paston with a little scroll of paper in his hand, written by him in English; part of this scroll was newly written, and he took ashes out of the chimney to dry it. The said Sir Thomas Howes asked what he had there. Paston said he had something that he would have given a hundred pounds to begin earlier. What the contents of the said scroll were the said Sir Thomas did not know at that time, until, on the Tuesday night after the decease of the said Fastolf, the said Paston being in a chamber in the said Caister Castle, called to him the said Sir Thomas, Friar John Brackley, a Minorite friar, Friar Clement Felmingham, an Austin friar and William Worcester, in the presence of various servants of the said Fastolf. He had a piece of paper in his hand, which he did not read, but folded it and put wax on it, and asked the two friars to put their seals on it; and Paston sealed it in the same way, asking the said Worcester to keep it that night until the following morning; and so he did, and then delivered it to the said Paston. After that the said Paston opened the said scroll, in the said Sir Thomas's presence, and it was read. And then the said Paston and the said friars informed the said Sir Thomas that among other matters there was contained in the said scroll a certain covenant which he had not heard about before, that the said Paston should have all the manors, lands and tenements of the said Fastolf in Norfolk, Suffolk and Norwich for four thousand marks, and that the said John Paston and the said Thomas and no other of the said Fastolf's executors should administer, receive and dispose of both his lands and goods during both their lives; and also the money that should come from the Fastolf lands by the sale of them should be administered and received and disposed of by the said Paston and Thomas only, and all the remaining co-executors should abstain from interfering in the disposal of the goods.'

143

Howes went on to describe how John Paston had tried to make an arrangement of this sort during Fastolf's lifetime, but said that Sir John Fastolf had reacted angrily to the suggestion. Yet Howes' story is a curious one, and does not really ring true. If forgery was being committed, why did Paston apparently do it so openly, unless it was a clumsy attempt to implicate all those present in the plot he had contrived? The formal sealing of the scroll on Tuesday night and its opening the following morning also seems difficult to explain. Howes also claimed that Paston had redrafted the will on subsequent occasions and had persuaded most of Fastolf's servants to swear to a false version of events. It is obvious that the household at Caister was in considerable confusion as Fastolf lay dying, and Howes' claim to know exactly where everyone was and what they were doing is over-confident. On the other hand, there are some telling points, such as the fact that Fastolf could only speak in a low whisper on the day he was said to have made the new will.

Howes' change of heart made it easier for Sir John's enemies to attack his title to the estates, as Sir John's authority was only equal to that of Howes in matters concerning the will. On October 10, Howes wrote to the archbishop of Canterbury, another of the original executors, explaining that he and Sir William Yelverton had been approached by the duke of Norfolk, with a view to the duke's purchasing Caister Castle from them as executors under the original will, and asking the archbishop to approve this deal. It was of course the duke's father who had seized Caister in 1461, and his son was now trying to acquire it by seemingly legal means. Sir John, short of money and in danger of losing the lawsuit over the will, was in no position to mount the necessary resistance from his own resources, but there was no one else to whom he could turn who could offer the necessary support. In early November the Pastons were expecting the duke to try to enforce his claim, and Sir John wrote to his brother describing the preparations he was making:

'*Right well-beloved brother*, I commend myself to you, letting you know that I have hired four reliable and trustworthy men to help Daubeney and you to keep the place at Caister, and to do whatever they are asked to do to safeguard or reinforce the said place. Besides, they are proven men, skilled in war and in deeds of arms: they are good at firing both guns and crossbows and can mend and string them, and can make bulwarks or anything that would strengthen the place; and they would keep watch and guard as necessary. They are sober and knowledgeable men, except for one who is bald, called William Percy, who is as good a man as any in the world, but is inclined to be a little drunken, but he is no brawler, but full of courtesy. The other three are named Peryn Sale, John Chapman, and Robert Jackson. The only thing is that no armour has come for them yet, but when it comes it will be sent to you. In the meanwhile, could you and Daubeney please provide some for them. They will also need a couple of beds; please get my mother to help you provide them until I come home. You will find them gentlemen and reassuring companions, who will stand their ground.

'I am sending you these men because the people round about you will be afraid to lose their goods if you learn that any attack is planned; so if such a thing happens, please take only a few of the local people and make sure that they are reliable, because otherwise they might discourage all the rest.

'And as for any letters from the king, he has promised not to send any; and if they do this unexpectedly, your answer shall be that the king has said that none were to be sent, so you can delay things until I hear of it, and I will soon arrange a remedy.'

Sir John's confidence in the king was not entirely rewarded, because early in January 1469 a writ came summoning him to appear before the king's council over the dispute between him and the duke, and ordering him to 'cease the riots and assemblies' he was making as a result of it.

Both the affairs of the Pastons and the political situation in 1469 are so complex, with a number of difficult crises running at the same time, that it is very difficult to trace them in sequence through the letters. For the Pastons there were four main concerns. The most important was the duke's claim to Caister, which came to a head in September, when the castle was starved into surrender despite a gallant defence by

John III. Allied to this were a further series of claims by the duke on Fastolf's lands, which resulted in the harrassment of tenants on various estates. Two projected marriages figured largely in this year: Sir John Paston became engaged to Lady Anne Haute, a relative of the earl of Oxford, an alliance which promised to bring reward of an effective political patron which the Pastons had lacked for so long. In sharp contrast, Sir John's sister Margery declared her intention of marrying the family's bailiff, Richard Calle, and eloped with him, much to her mother's fury and the disgust of the socially ambitious Sir John. Finally, there was the long drawn out battle in the law courts over Fastolf's will: Thomas Howes died early in the year, but Sir John was still unable to make headway, and had to concern himself with his father's will as well.

All this took place against the background of a political crisis. Warwick, whose discontent with Edward we have already noted, decided early in 1469 that the time had come for action against the Woodville family in order to bring the king to heel. In June and July matters came to a head: by June 20, Warwick, with the support of Louis XI, had raised a large force and seized London, while the king offered no effective opposition to the coup, and was captured by Archbishop Neville at Olney in Buckinghamshire. The leaders of the Woodville family were executed outside Bristol, and a parliament was summoned at York to ratify Warwick's actions. But Warwick was unable to keep order, and it was at this point, in September, that the duke of Norfolk attacked Caister. Edward managed to gather his supporters at Pontefract, and by the end of the year had re-established himself in London. Although he was apparently reconciled to Warwick, the latter was still plotting against him and was now definitely aiming at the restoration of Henry VI.

Against such a background, the old problems of the Pastons reappear as well, more acute than ever, but with even less chance of resolution. In March, Margaret wrote to Sir John complaining that Norfolk's men were now harrassing the tenants of Heynford and elsewhere, and indeed the rival trustees of Fastolf's lands had sold not only Caister but a whole group of other manors to the duke. On the other hand, Margaret wrote hopefully of a settlement over the manor at

Hellesdon where the duchess of Suffolk was maintaining her husband's old claim. But she was doomed to disappointment: when the king came to Norfolk in June, Sir John and his uncle William arranged for the king to ride past Hellesdon to see the ruins, and the duchess stayed well away in Oxfordshire lest the king should call her to account for the damage done there.

But John III reported the occasion a few days later:

'The king rode through Hellesdon Warren towards Walsingham, and Thomas Wingfield promised me that he would find some means for my lord of Gloucester and himself to show the king the lodge which was pulled down, and that they would tell him about the breaking down of the place. Contrary to this, and to the encouragement I had from my lord Scales, Sir John Woodville and Thomas Wingfield, my uncle William says that the king himself told him when he had ridden past the lodge in Hellesdon Warren that he thought that it could just as well have fallen down by itself as have been pulled down; if it had been pulled down, he said we could have put in a claim about it when the judges of *oyer et terminer* sat at Norwich in his presence. My uncle says that he answered the king by saying that you trusted in his good grace to make an agreement with both the dukes [of Suffolk and Norfolk] by negotiation. He says that the king replied that he would neither speak for you nor negotiate, but would let the law take its course; and with that, he says, they left. By my faith, unless the lord treasurer supports you better than he did us here, you will have little help from that quarter; so pursue your claims actively, for you need to do so: for all their pleasant words, I cannot see what good their efforts in this county have done. Do not be too hasty until you are sure of your lands, but press on with the lawsuits. Until those are settled, you will have little help, as I see it.'

Lord Scales had tried to intervene on Sir John's behalf in the even more difficult matter of Caister: for he was both a member of the duke of Norfolk's council, and a prospective relative by marriage of Sir John. We know little of Sir John's engagement to Lady Anne Haute, except that it took place early in 1469, and is spoken of as a definite agreement by Lord Scales in April. Earlier in that month Margaret Paston knew of it but was unsure of the details: she wrote to Sir John asking for more news:

'I have no definite news about your engagement, but if you are engaged, I pray God send you joy and honour together, and I believe you will have them if what is said of her is true. Before God you are as firmly bound to her as if you were married; and therefore I command you on pain of losing my blessing that you are as true to her as if she was married to you in church, and you will have all the more grace and better fortune in everything else. Do not be in too much of a hurry to get married until you are sure of your estates, for you must remember how much you will have to spend, and if you cannot maintain that kind of expenditure, it would be a great dishonour. So do your best to get releases from the lords, and be more secure in possession of your lands before you get married.'

We know very little about Anne Haute, except that she was closely related to the Woodvilles, and the match seems to have been one of political expediency. Sir John himself only mentions her when he is doubtful about going through with the marriage, though it may be that his caution was due in part to his mother's warnings about the precarious state of his finances.

In the same letter, Margaret also refers to another family matter:

'Also, I would like you to arrange for your sister to be with my lady of Oxford or with my lady of Bedford or in some other respectable place, as you think best, and I will help pay for her keep, because we are both weary of each other. I shall tell you more when I speak to you. Please do your duty here, if you can, for my comfort and welfare and your good name, for various reasons which I will explain to you later.'

The 'various reasons' emerged soon enough. In May John III wrote to his brother, who had evidently discovered what was going on. 'R.C.' is Richard Calle, the family's bailiff since at least 1460. He must have been at least in his early thirties, possibly older, while Margery was about twenty.

'Sir, please realise that I understand from the letter that you sent me by Juddy that you have heard of R.C.'s plots, which he is making with the agreement of our ungracious sister; but as far as they wrote that they have my good will in the matter, saving your reverence, they are lying, because they never spoke to me about it, nor did anyone else on their behalf. Lovell once asked me whether I knew what was going on between R.C. and my sister. I suspect that Calle put him up to it, for when I asked whether C. had asked him to put that question or not, he tried to get out of it by humming and hawing. But I would not take this for an answer, so in the end, he told me that his eldest son had asked him to find out whether R.C. was sure of her or not, for he said he knew a good match for her. But I know he lied, for he is entirely on R.C.'s side in that business; so, in order not to give them any encouragement, I replied that even if my father (on whom God have mercy) were alive and had consented to it, and my mother and both of you as well, he would never have my good will to make my sister sell candles and mustard in Framlingham; and so, with more talk which would take too long to write to you, we parted.

'Just as you ask my pardon in your letter for not sending the things I sent you money for, I ask your pardon for being so stupid as to trouble you with such simple matters, knowing the great and weighty affairs you have to deal with, but need compelled me, because there is nothing of the kind in this part of the world.

'Also, you were kind enough to send a message to Richard Calle to give me money, but, God help me, I will ask nothing of him for myself, nor have I had anything from him, nor from anyone except my own men, since you left; but what little I could spare of my own I have given to Daubeney for the household or used it to pay men's wages for you. So anyone who tells you that I have spent any of your money since you left must write you a different set of accounts, except in meat and drink, because I eat like a horse on purpose, in order to eat you out of house and home; but there is no need for that, for you never set foot in your home, and therefore, God help me, the company here think you have forgotten all of us. If anything is badly managed when you come home, blame yourself for lack of supervision.

'I am reliably informed, by a message from my lord's household, that this Whitsun my lord's council will be at Framlingham, and they intend to hold courts here at Caister and at all other manors which were Sir John F's, bought by them from Yelverton and T.H., on whom God have mercy. It is too late to send to you for advice as to what I should do, so if I do well I ask no thanks, and if I do badly, blame the fault on our lack of wisdom. But I intend to follow the first rule of hawking, and hold fast if I can. But, God help me, if they pull down the house about our ears, I do not blame them, though I will prevent them if I can. For, by God who redeemed me, the best earl in England would not deal with my lord and lady [of Norfolk] in the way you do, without making some direct approach to them. God help me, whoever advises you to act as you do is not your friend.

'If I may, I trust to God that I shall see you about Midsummer or before, for indeed I think you intend to wait until Easter before you come home; all your servants here think you do not intend to have anything more to do with them, but are going to leave them as hostages for my lord of Norfolk.

'Please arrange which inn my brother Edmund is to enter, for he is wasting his time completely here, I promise you. Please send word by the next messenger who comes, and I will either send him or bring him with me to London.

'Also, sir, we poor penniless men of Caister have broken three or four steel bows; so we beg you that if there is any very skilful maker of steel bows in London, you will let me know, and I will send you the bows which are broken; they are your own great bow, Robert Jackson's bow and John Pampyng's bow. These three have fired so many shots that they will not fire crossbow bolts until they are repaired. Please find a way of offering a reasonable compromise to my lord so that he and my lady will realise that you want to gain his favour. I promise you it will help both you and your tenants. And God preserve you.'

J.P.

Despite the opposition of Margery's family, the lovers remained steadfast: at some time during the summer Richard Calle wrote to Margery, and, in a letter which is the only one of their correspondence to survive – probably because it was intercepted – he describes their situation:

'*My own lady and mistress*, and indeed my true wife before God, I commend myself to you with a very sad heart as a man who cannot be cheerful and will not be until things stand otherwise with us than they do now. This life that we lead now pleases neither God nor the world, considering the great bond of matrimony that is made between us, and also the great love that has been, and I trust still is, between us, and which for my part was never greater. So I pray that Almighty God will comfort us as soon as it pleases him, for we who ought by rights to be most together are most apart; it seems a thousand years since I last spoke to you. I would rather be with you than all the wealth in the world. Alas, also, good lady, those who keep us apart like this, scarcely realise what they are doing: those who hinder matrimony are cursed in church four times a year. It makes many men think that they can stretch a point of conscience in other matters as well as this one. But whatever happens, lady, bear it as you have done and be as cheerful as you can, for be sure, lady, that God in the long run will of his righteousness help his servants who mean to be true and want to live according to his laws.

'I realise, lady, that you have had as much sorrow on my account as any gentlewoman has ever had in this world; I wish to God that all the sorrow you have had had fallen on me, so that you were freed of it; for indeed, lady, it kills me to hear that you are being treated otherwise than you should be. This is a painful life we lead; I cannot imagine that we live like this without God being displeased by it.

'You will want to know that I sent you a letter from London by my lad, and he told me he could not speak to you, because so great a watch was kept on both you and him. He told me that John Thresher came to him in your name, and said that you had sent him to my lad for a letter or token which you thought I had sent you; but he did not trust him and would not deliver anything to him. After that he brought a ring, saying that you sent it to him, commanding him to deliver the letter or token to him, which I gather since then from my lad was not sent by you, but was a plot of my mistress [i.e. Margaret Paston] and James Gloys. Alas, what do they intend? I suppose they think we are not engaged; and if this is the case I am very surprised, for they are not being sensible, remembering how plainly I told my mistress about everything at the beginning, and I think you have told her so too, if you have done as you should. And if you have denied it, as I have been told you have done, it was done neither with a good conscience nor to the pleasure of God, unless you did it for fear and to please those who were with you at the time. If this was the reason you did it, it was justified, considering how insistently you were called on to deny it; and you were told many untrue stories about me, which, God knows, I was never guilty of.

'My lad told me that your mother asked him if he had brought any letter to you, and she accused him falsely of many other things; among other things, she said to him in the end that I would not tell her about it at the beginning, but she expected that I would at the ending. As for that, God knows that she knew about it first from me and no one else. I do not know what my mistress means, for in truth there is no other gentlewoman alive who I respect more than her and whom I would be more sorry to displease, saving only yourself who by right I ought to cherish and love best, for I am bound to do so by God's law and will do so while I live, whatever may come of it. I expect that if you tell them the sober truth, they will not damn their souls for our sake. Even if I tell them the truth they will not believe me as much as they would you. And so, good lady, for reverence of God be plain with them and tell the truth, and if they will not agree, let it be between them, God and the devil; and as for the peril we should be in, I pray God it may lie on them and not on us. I am very sad and sorry when I think of their attitude. God guide them and send them rest and peace.

'I am very surprised that they are as concerned about this affair as I gather that they are, in view of the fact that nothing can be done about it, and that I deserve better; from any point of view there should be no obstacles to it. Also their honour does not depend on your marriage, but in their own marriage [ie Sir John's]; I pray God send them a marriage which will be to their honour, to God's pleasure and to their heart's ease, for otherwise it would be a great pity.

'Mistress, I am frightened of writing to you, for I understand that you have showed the letters that I have sent you before to others, but I beg you, let no one see this letter. As soon as you have read it, burn it, for I would not want anyone to see it. You have had nothing in writing from me for two years, and I will not send you any more: so I leave everything to your wisdom.

'Almighty Jesu preserve, keep and give you your heart's desire, which I am sure will please God. This letter was written with as great difficulty as I ever wrote anything in my life, for I have been very ill, and am not yet really recovered, may God amend it.'

Matters came to a head in early September, when, probably at Calle's request, the bishop of Norwich intervened in the matter, and summoned both him and Margery to be questioned about the engagement. In medieval church law, a spoken promise of marriage, *per verba de praesenti*, was as binding as a full marriage ceremony, and it seems that Richard and Margery had indeed exchanged such vows. Agnes and Margaret were both involved in this family crisis, and Margaret reported what had happened to Sir John on September 10:

'Last Thursday my mother and I were with my lord of Norwich and asked him to do nothing more in the affair until you and my brother and the others who were your father's executors could be here together, because they were in charge of her as well as I. And he said plainly that he had been asked so often before to examine her, that he could not and would not delay it any longer, and charged me, on pain of cursing, that she should not be held back but should appear before him the next day. And I said as plainly that I would neither bring her nor send her; and then he said he would send for her himself, and charged me to see that she would be at liberty to come when he sent for her. And he said that he would indeed be as sorry for her if she did not do well as he would be if she were a close relation of his, both for my mother's sake and mine and other friends of hers; for he knew that her behaviour had grieved us greatly.

'My mother and I told him that we never heard her say that she had spoken to him in terms that would bind them to each other, but that both were free to choose. Then he said he would talk to her as best he could before he examined her; and various people told me afterwards that he did this as well and as plainly as if she had been a close relation; but it would take too long to write about it now. I will let you know later who was behind it all. The chancellor was not so guilty as I thought he was.

'On Friday the bishop sent Ashfield and others who are very sorry about her behaviour to fetch her. And the bishop spoke to her frankly, and reminded her of her birth, relations and friends, and what friends she might have if she followed their advice; and if she did not follow it, what dishonour and shame and loss it would be to her, and how they would forsake her and would not help or comfort her. He said that he had heard that she loved someone whom her friends did not want her to marry, and told her to be very careful what she did. He said that he wanted to know what words she had said to him, and whether they were binding vows of matrimony or not. And she repeated what she had said, and boldly said that if these words did not make things sure, she would make it sure before she left; for she said that she thought that she was bound in conscience, whatever the words were. These foolish words grieve me and her grandmother as much as everything else together. Then the bishop and the chancellor both said that neither I nor any friends of hers would take her in. Then Calle was examined separately by himself, to see that her words and his agreed, as well as the time and place when it was supposed to have been done. Then the bishop said that he thought other things might be found against him which would hinder the marriage, and therefore he would not be too hasty in giving sentence; he said he would postpone judgement until the Wednesday or Thursday after Michaelmas, and so it is delayed until then.

'They wanted to have their wishes carried out at once, but the bishop said he would do as he had said. I was with my mother at her house when she was examined, and when I heard how she had behaved, I ordered my servants that she was not to be allowed in my house. I had warned her, and she might have taken heed if she had been well-disposed. I sent messages to one or two others that they should not let her in if she came. She was brought back to my house to be let in, and James Gloys told those who brought her that I had ordered them all that she should not be allowed in. So my lord of Norwich has lodged her at Roger Best's, to stay there until the day in question; God knows it is much against his will and his wife's, but they dare not do otherwise. I am sorry that they are burdened with her, but I am better off with her there than somewhere else, because he and his wife are sober and well-disposed to us, and she will not be allowed to play the good-for-nothing there.

'Please do not take all this too hard, because I know that it is a matter close to your heart, as it is to mine and other people's; but remember, as I do, that we have only lost a good-for-nothing in her, and take it less to heart: if she had been any good, whatever might have happened, things would not have been as they are, for even if he were dead now, she would never be as close to me as she was. As for the divorce you wrote to me about, I understand what you meant, but I order you on pain of losing my blessing that you do not do anything, or get anyone else to do anything, that would offend God and your conscience: for if you do, God will take vengeance on you, and you would put yourself and others in great danger. You can be sure that she will regret her foolishness afterwards, and I pray to God that she does. Please, for my sake, be cheerful about all this. I trust that God will help us; may he do so in all our affairs.'

The bishop's judgement was that Margery and Richard's vows were binding, but Sir John still hoped to prevent the match. In October he wrote to Margaret asking her to get the bishop to delay the wedding until Christmas, by which time he hoped to have found a way of stopping it. However, the marriage went ahead, and Margery disappears from the letters, though some kind of reconciliation must have taken place, because in 1482 Margaret left £20 to John Calle 'son of my daughter Margery' in her will. Calle himself, after a period out of favour, continued to be employed by the Pastons, apparently still being in John III's service as late as 1503.

Meanwhile, matters had also come to a head at Caister: on August 21 the long-awaited attack began, at a time when central authority was at its weakest. Sir John was either in London or with the king when the siege began, and it was John III who was in command, assisted by Daubeney and the hired soldiers. On August 31, one of the duke of Norfolk's captains, Sir John Heveningham, spoke to Margaret Paston at Norwich, but evidently had no brief to open negotiations. Margaret felt that the eldest son was not playing his part and complained that she had 'no good answer' from him about the situation: 'it grieves me very much that I have sent you so many messages and have got such feeble replies.' Sir John was in fact doing what he was best at: trying to raise support for his cause among the magnates of the court, and getting letters from the duke of Clarence, who was Warwick's favourite and the king's brother. But he failed to realise that this time Norfolk did not care twopence for such letters, knowing that the great lords and the king had their own intrigues to keep them occupied. The only remedy was force, and he could not command either men or money for an instant attempt to relieve the besiegers. Margaret Paston had grasped the situation much more clearly, as is shown by her letter of September 12:

'I greet you well, and let you know that your brother and his company stand in great danger at Caister and lack provisions; Daubeney and Berney are dead and various others badly hurt.

'They are running out of gunpowder and arrows, and the place is much broken down by the other side's guns: so unless they have help quickly, they are likely to lose both their lives and the place, and it will be as great a dishonour to you as ever happened to any gentleman, for every man in the country is astonished that you allow them to be in such great danger for so long without help or any other remedy.

'The duke has been all the more fervently set on getting the place, and more fierce since Writtle, my lord of Clarence's man, was there, than he was before; and he has sent for all his tenants from everywhere, and others, to be at Caister next Thursday morning, so that there is likely to be the greatest multitude of people there then that came there so far. They want to make a great assault, for they have sent for guns to King's Lynn and other places by the seaside, so that with their great multitude of guns, along with other artillery and ordnance, no one will dare to appear in the place. They will keep them so busy with their great crowd of people that it will not be in their power to hold it against them unless God helps them or they have help very quickly from you.'

She goes on to suggest that he gets letters from the duke of Clarence or the archbishop of York, and even moots the idea that he should make over a life interest in Caister to the earl of Oxford in order to save his title to the freehold. Sir John replied three days later.

'*Mother*, last Saturday Daubeney and Berney were alive and cheerful, and I do not think anyone has come out of the place since that time who could have given you certain news of their deaths. As for the fierceness of the duke and his men since Writtle departed, I think it was agreed that a truce and abstinence of war was agreed before he left which will last till next Monday. By that time I think a truce will be made until a week from that day, by which time I hope things will have improved.

'You wrote to me that I should get letters from my lords of Clarence and York, but they are not here; and if they wrote to him, as they have done twice, it would be to no effect. To organise those letters and a relief force are two separate matters, for when the relief force is ready all the expense has been incurred – if I have to rescue the place before those who should do it arrive, it would cost a thousand crowns and as much again afterwards; and it would be hard for me to take this course when I could do it some other way. But as for saying that they shall be rescued if all the land I have in England, and friends, may do it, they shall indeed, if God is friendly, and it shall be carried out as soon as it can be done in good order. The greatest need on earth is for money and some friends and neighbours to help; so please send me encouragement by letting me know what money you can manage to get or raise on security or by mortgage or sale of estates, and how many people your friends and mine could raise at short notice, and send me word as quickly as is needed.

'But mother, I feel from your letter that you think that I would not do my duty unless you sent me some bad news; if I needed a letter to urge me on in this crisis, I would indeed be too slow a fellow. But, mother, I assure you I have heard ten times worse news since the siege began, than by any letter you wrote me, and sometimes I have heard very good news. But this I assure you: no one in Caister has less rest than I, nor runs greater risks. Whether I have good news or bad, I take God to witness that I have done my duty as I would be served in a similar situation, and will do until there is an end to it.'

Three days later, on September 18, Sir John wrote encouragingly to John III, promising action within a week or a fortnight. But the crisis came sooner, as his mother feared: by September 25, John III had been forced to surrender, accepting a safe-conduct from the duke of Norfolk for himself and the garrison. Even the safe-conduct was only granted, as the duke put it, at the request of the archbishop of Canterbury, the duke of Clarence and 'other lords of our blood' as well as at his wife's especial request. Under the circumstances, John III's letter to his brother written just after the siege had ended, is remarkably forgiving, in view of Sir John's total failure to organise any help at all:

'*Right worshipful sir*, I commend myself to you. As for the certainty of the surrender of Caister, John Chapman can tell you as well as I can how we were forced to do so. As for John Chapman and his three companions, I have arranged for each of them to be paid 40s out of the money they had from you and Daubeney: that is enough for the period for which they have served you. Please thank them for it, for in truth they deserve it as much as anyone who ever lived; and as for money, you need not give them any unless you want to, for they are pleased with their wages.

'Writtle promised me he would send you the details of the terms. We were driven to come to terms for lack of victuals, gunpowder, low morale and lack of certain relief.

'If you want me to come to you, send me word and I will arrange to stay with you for two or three days. In truth, rewarding the people who have been with me during the siege has put me in great hardship for money.

'God preserve you and please be of good heart until I speak to you; I trust to God that I can put you at ease over some things.'

J. Paston

There was little that the Pastons could do about the loss of Caister, but the news did have repercussions elsewhere. Apart from Sir William Yelverton, who was involved in litigation with the Pastons over the will, the only impartial surviving executor was Bishop Wainfleet of Winchester. With the archbishop of Canterbury's consent – for wills were an ecclesiastical matter – Wainfleet now put forward proposals to settle the whole question, in view of the great damage that was being done to the estate for want of a clear title: Hellesdon and Drayton had been ruined, and now Caister itself was lost. Wainfleet's move was perhaps rather belated, and, as we shall see, he had schemes of his own in mind; but it did lead to a solution. The first word that something was afoot came in a letter to John III from Sir John in February 1470, which opened with various business matters, and continued with gossip:

'As for Mistress Katherine Dudley, I have recommended you to her many times, and she is far from displeased by it. She does not care how many gentlemen love her – she is full of love. I have pursued the matter without your knowledge, as I told her. She replies that she will not take anyone for two years, and I believe her, for I think she leads a life that she can be content with. I think she will have to work hard to save her soul for the next two years.

'Please speak to Harcourt of the Abbey for a little clock which I sent him by James Gresham to mend, and get it from him and send it to me. As for money for his work, he has another clock of mine which Sir Thomas Lyndes, God have his soul, gave me. He may keep that till I pay him. This clock belongs to my lord archbishop, but do not let him know that, and get it carried here carefully as you think best.

'There is a compromise offered by means of my lord of Winchester between Sir William Yelverton and me, and both Sir William Yelverton and I agree to abide by his award; so I hope this law-term to get a compromise and an end to the case; and, in confidence, I am not afraid of the award. I cannot put my hopes and the reasons for them in writing – as long as Sir William Yelverton abides by what he has said; and if he does not, then he is deceived, for my lord of Winchester has taken over the administration of Sir John Fastolf's will, and Sir William Yelverton is excluded. Sir William Yelverton does not know this, and there is no need to tell him. But you can say this to William Yelverton, who has before now pretended that he meant well and said that he wanted us to be reconciled, that you understand that an agreement has been made between him and me, and that you hope to God there will be an end to the case and we can all be good friends again; and say that you understand that Heydon will do his best to prevent it, for when all is said and done he does not like Sir W. Yelverton, nor me neither, and he has laughed at both of us for a long time. If we two could agree, neither of us would need to deal with him in future, for he does not love either of us but has a longstanding grudge which makes him hate both of us. Moreover, he himself has said of Sir William Yelverton that he has not behaved wisely and has risked his livelihood out of hatred of me; he should have known what he was doing, but, Heydon said, he was not wise, seeing that if I had won against him in Chancery he would indeed have been undone.

'But I assure you that I do not care whether the agreement takes effect or not, because other things are about to happen, by the grace of God; they are too secret to write about. Do not let anyone know about this business except our mother and yourself, not even James Gloys or anyone else.'

John III was doubtful about the settlement, almost as a postscript to his reply to Sir John's letter on March 1, he wrote:

'As for the bishop of Winchester, W. Worcester told my mother that he had taken charge ten days before Pampyng came home, but he thinks that the bishop will be against you, so much so that he advised my mother to tell you to petition my lord cardinal that the said bishop should not be allowed to take administration.'

Meanwhile, the political crisis of the previous year continued. Warwick, despite outward appearances, was now more determined than ever to overthrow Edward, who seemed to have escaped his clutches once more. He engineered rebellions in Lincolnshire and Yorkshire, by fomenting local discontent.

Edward acted promptly enough to prevent the rebellion becoming serious: the rebels tried to join Warwick, who was near Leicester, but were defeated by Edward near Stamford, in a battle called 'Lose-Cote Field' because the rebels stripped off their jackets in their haste to escape. The leaders of the Lincolnshire rebellion were captured, and implicated both Warwick and Clarence. Sir John learnt of all this from an anonymous correspondent on March 27:

'The king came to Grantham and stayed there all Thursday, and there were beheaded there Sir Thomas Dalalaunde and one John Neille, a great captain; and on the next Monday he was at Doncaster, and there Sir Robert Wells and another great captain were beheaded. Then the king had word that the duke of Clarence and the earl of Warwick were at Esterfeld twenty miles from Doncaster; on the Tuesday, at nine by the bell, the king took to the field and mustered his people, and it was said that there were never seen in England so many fine men and so well arrayed in the field. And my lord had an honourable company with him, as good as any lord's, and the king thanked my lord warmly for it.

'And when the duke of Clarence and the earl of Warwick heard that the king was coming towards them, they left in a hurry and went to Manchester in Lancashire, hoping to get help and support from Lord Stanley; but in the end they got little assistance, so the king was told. Men say they went westward; some think they went to London. When the king heard they had separated he went to York and came there the following Thursday. All the gentlemen of the shire came to him there, and on Lady Day he made Percy earl of Northumberland, and he who had been earl was made Marquis Montagu. So the king intends to come south. God send him good fortune. Written the 27th day of March.'

The king was soon on the track of the rebels, but despite forced marches which took him and his army down to Exeter in under three weeks, Clarence and Warwick escaped across the Channel, and attempted to enter Calais, held by a supporter of theirs. But they were refused entry, and had to take refuge with Louis XI. On July 24, Warwick and Queen Margaret were reconciled, and plans were laid for a Lancastrian invasion of England with French support.

For the Pastons, the spring and summer were a period of relative peace, though a new family quarrel emerged. William, Sir John's uncle, had always felt that John I had dealt with him unfairly over his inheritance; and now that he had married the daughter of the late duke of Somerset, Lady Anne Beaufort, he began to press his claims, perhaps in order to find money to maintain his new position in the world. His tactics were like those employed by Yelverton, over the Fastolf property but with the added twist that the more Sir John was involved in lawsuits the more likely he was to want to sell property, which in many cases he could only do with William's consent. A letter from John III to Sir John on May 25 outlines some of the problems:

'Indeed, I assure you that I never saw my mother more disturbed by anything in her life than she was when she read the note in which you gave me warning that Parker had started an action against you and me, for she thinks that it has been arranged by my uncle William to make you sell your land. She ordered me to send you word that if you sell any land instead of paying your debts with the goods that my lord archbishop owes you, if any law in England can keep you out of her land, she swears by the faith she owes to God that she will deprive you of twice as much land as you sell. So I would put pressure on my lord the archbishop, for you do not have to ruin yourself for his sake.

'Please see that Parker does me no harm. As for my Uncle W., I cannot make him send you the list of the stuff of yours that he has. He says he will, but does not produce it. He and I have fallen out badly over some business between Lovell and Joan Walsham and her sister. Lovell has bought Joan Walsham's part of her estates and has married her to a knave, and as my uncle W. has often spoken to my mother and myself to get me to deliver to Lovell Joan Walsham's deeds which I have in my keeping; and because I will not deliver the deeds to Lovell, he says he will strip me of the manor of Swainsthorpe. . .'

In June, there were further threats of action by William, who had evidently got old Agnes Paston on his side. He, Lady Anne and Agnes were said to be coming to London to bring a case which would transfer Agnes' lands to William from Sir John. It was to be the beginning of yet another long-drawn-out lawsuit. For the moment, however, there was little to be done, and John III proposed to go on pilgrimage on foot to Canterbury the following week. However, just as this new lawsuit threatened, the old wrangle over the Fastolf estates was settled, by an agreement dated July 14. By this, Wainfleet was to take over everything except Caister, Hellesdon, Drayton, some two or three lesser manors and some holdings in Norwich; Caister was to go to Sir John as his exclusive property, but the proceeds of the other manors were to be divided equally between Wainfleet and Sir John. Instead of the college at Caister – and here Wainfleet's interest in the deal emerges – seven priests and seven poor scholars were to be provided for at Wainfleet's newly founded Magdalen College at Oxford, 'to pray for the souls of the said John Fastolf and of Dame Millicent his wife, his friends and benefactors'.

The shadow of political events now loomed large. On August 5, Sir John wrote to his younger brother:

'Please be ready, for affairs are coming to a head for both you and yours, as well as us and ours. As for news, my lord archbishop is at the Moor, but various of the king's servants are left there with him, and I understand that he has permission to stay there until he is sent for. Many people have risen in the north, so that Percy is unable to hold out against them; and so the king has sent for his retainers to come to him, for he wants to go and put down the revolt. Some say that the king will come back to London very soon; and it is said that Courtenay has landed in Devonshire and controls it.

'The lords Clarence and Warwick will try to land in England any day, so people fear. . .'

It was in fact September 9 before Clarence and Warwick landed, delayed in France by a blockade by the English and Burgundian fleets. When these were scattered by a storm, the invaders were able to cross. Landing at Dartmouth and Plymouth, they found the south at their mercy, because Edward had gone north to deal with the rebellion there. The west country had strongly Lancastrian sympathies, and recruiting proved easy: as the dukes marched into the midlands in search of Edward, their forces grew rapidly. They were joined by the earl of Shrewsbury and Lord Stanley, and when they reached Coventry, news came that Montagu, who had been given a marquisate in exchange for the earldom of Northumberland, had taken his revenge by deserting Edward at the critical moment. Edward, fearing that Montagu would actually turn and attack him, fled to East Anglia and, taking ship at King's Lynn, made for Burgundy, reaching Bruges in early October. At the same time, Henry VI was back in London as king of England, with Warwick as his chief supporter.

The Pastons, who had been unwaveringly Yorkist till now, changed sides at the restoration of Henry VI. This was due to their own local situation rather than any change of principle. Their erstwhile patron, now their greatest enemy, the duke of Norfolk, was firmly Yorkist, and they hoped, by following the earl of Oxford into the Lancastrian camp, to have their revenge on him, as John III wrote to his mother on October 12:

'I trust that we shall very soon do very well in all our affairs, for my lady of Norfolk has promised to be governed by my lord of Oxford in everything that concerns my brothers and me. As for my lord of Oxford, he is more favourable to me in many things than I could indeed hope for: for he sent John Bernard to my lady of Norfolk about my business alone, and for no other reason, without my knowledge or request. When he sent him to her, I was in London and he was at Colchester, which shows that he remembers me. The duke and duchess petition him as humbly as ever I did them, so that the lord of Oxford will control them and theirs at their request and by their own arrangements.

'As for the offices you wrote to my brother about, and to me, they are not for poor men; but I hope we shall get other suitable posts, because my master the earl of Oxford tells me to ask for whatever I want. I think my brother Sir John will have the constableship of Norwich Castle and £20 a year as his fee; all the lords have agreed to it.

'News: the earl of Worcester is likely due to die today, or at latest tomorrow. John Pilkington, Master W. Hatcliffe and Fowler have been captured and are in the castle of Pontefract; they are likely to die soon, if they are not already dead. Sir T. Montgomery and John Donne are captured. What will happen to them I cannot say. The ex-queen and the duchess of Bedford are in the sanctuary at Westminster. The bishop of Ely and other bishops are in St Martin's. When I hear more, I shall send you more news.'

Sir John was equally anxious to make the most of his connections with the earl of Oxford, and on November 15, he wrote to his brother:

'Brother, please remember me to my good lord the earl of Oxford; I told my lord that I would wait on his lordship in Norfolk, and I would rather have done so than lost a hundred pounds; but in all good faith the business which I told my lord I thought would delay me was not finished till yesterday, so give that as a reason. And also since All Soul's day, I have been unwell every other day and have not recovered. Since that day I have gone round with a stick in Westminster Hall and everywhere else, like a ghost, people say, as though I rose out of the earth rather than from a fair lady's bed; and I am still like that, though I hope I shall get better. So I beg his lordship to pardon me, and I will make amends twice over, for if you had hired me to ride to Norfolk for 500 marks I would not have gone so willingly as I would have at this time to wait his lordship; and I would have liked to be there so that my lord could know how much service I might have done in that part of the world.'

If the family's political futures looked bright, their finances were in a bad way. On October 28, Margaret wrote to John sending him twenty pounds' worth of silver plate to sell, which was apparently a family heirloom, and warning him:

'Beware how you spend it; use it only to settle such debts as you are in danger for, or in pursuit of your affairs; for unless you pay more attention to your expenses, you will bring great shame on yourself and your friends, and impoverish them so that none of us will be able to help each other, to the great encouragement of our enemies.

'Those who claim to be your friends in this part of the world realise in what great danger and need you stand, both from various of your friends and from your enemies. It is rumoured that I have parted with so much to you that I cannot help either you or any of my friends, which is no honour to us and causes people to esteem us less. At the moment it means that I must disperse my household and lodge somewhere, which I would be very loath to do if I were free to choose. It has caused a great deal of talk in this town and I would not have needed to do it if I had held back when I could. So for God's sake pay attention and be careful from now on, for I have handed over to you both my own property and your father's, and have held nothing back, either for myself or for his sake. I think that things are going all the worse because of this: it is a great shame that he was so honourably buried and since then his bequests have not been carried out and little has been done to carry out his wishes; and now, although I want to do so, I have nothing at all besides my estates I can decently raise any money on, and my estates are not in good shape; I am inclined to take Mautby in hand, and to start farming there, and I do not know whether it will be profitable. The rent-collector owes me £80 or more; and I do not know when I shall get it. So do not be more ready to spend money because you expect me to help you, because from now on I want to get myself out of the debts I have got into for your sake and carry out the wishes of your father and those who gave me my possessions. For until I do so, I know for certain that I shall lack grace and displease God, who have you in his keeping.

'I am sending you two pieces of cloth for shirts, each three yards long and the finest to be had in this town. I would have had them made here, but it would have been too long before you would have had them. Your aunt or some other good woman will make them as a kindness to you. Thank you for the gown you gave me: I hope I shall look respectable in it on All Saint's day. For reverence of God, take care and pay attention to what is written in this letter.

'Tell your brother that I have no money as yet that I can send him for the sarcenet and damasks which I spoke to him about. As for the damask, that can wait till next year, but as for the sarcenet, I would like to have it if possible before I go to my estates. Let your brother see this letter. As for your sister, I can send you no good news of her. God make her a good woman.'

By your mother

Two weeks later, Margaret wrote again, with more serious news about her husband's will:

'This is to let you know that I am sending you by the bearer of this letter £40 in gold coin, which I have borrowed for you on pledge, because I would not take the money laid aside for you at Norwich; for, so I am told by the chancellor, Master John Smith, and others, we have all been cursed for administering a dead man's goods without licence or authority, and I think matters are going all the worse with us because of it. For the reverence of God, get a licence from my lord of Canterbury, to ease my conscience and yours, to administer goods to the value of three or four hundred marks, and explain to him how your estates have been in such trouble these past two years that you could get nothing at all from them, nor can take anything now without hurting your tenants. They have been so harrassed by unjust means before now, and you have so much important business in hand, that you cannot afford to be forebearing with them or keep your rights without using your father's goods for a time. This I hope, will ease our conscience in respect of what we have administered and spent before; because we have no more money to pay off this £40 and all other charges than the £47 which you and your uncle know about, which is laid aside at Norwich.'

Matters did improve the following month: the new political situation made the duke of Norfolk anxious to avoid trouble with those who had successfully put Henry VI back on the throne, and, under circumstances about which we know nothing, he restored Caister to the Pastons. However, although the castle itself was returned, all their goods had been taken, and the place was stripped: the glass windows (which would at this period have been made so that they could be easily removed) had gone, twenty-five locks, lead from the roof and the kitchen equipment had all gone, as well as the guns and armaments and the furniture.

In February 1471, another old quarrel seemed to be settled, when Paston won the case against Yelverton and Jenney, and Fastolf's disputed will was declared genuine: but by now, under the terms of the agreement with Bishop Wainfleet, he was unable to benefit from it, and indeed signed a new document specifically stating that he would not go back on the settlement with Wainfleet because of the result of the case. But once again, the course of political events changed all this, and dashed the Pastons' rising hopes. Edward IV had found ready support at the Burgundian court, though Charles was unable to spare more than a handful of men. He also made an alliance with the powerful commercial league known as the Hanse, an association of merchant towns in Germany and the Baltic: in return for a restoration of their old trading privileges in England, they provided him with fourteen ships. On March 14, Edward, with between one and two thousand men, arrived off the Yorkshire coast. It was a small force, and its chance of success must have seemed remote; but the Lancastrians had not established firm control of England, and were beginning to quarrel among themselves. Warwick and Clarence were at loggerheads, and Queen Margaret had still not returned from France. Her absence was to prove fatal. The powerful lords in the north who could have crushed Edward as soon as he landed stood aside, saying, when summoned by Warwick, that they were awaiting Queen Margaret: Edward entered York, and although he had difficulty in recruiting more supporters, the neutrality of those who should have been his opponents was almost as valuable. By the end of March, he had raised enough men to challenge Warwick at Coventry; but Warwick, never a bold general, stayed inside the city walls. Edward took Warwick Castle instead, and at the same time Clarence returned to his brother's camp, a severe blow to Lancastrian morale.

Early in April, still unable to lure Warwick into battle despite a repeated challenge, Edward decided to make for London. Although Henry VI himself was in the city, the Londoners opened their gates to Edward on April 11, and Edward thus captured at one stroke the capital and his rival for the throne. Warwick was now isolated: he had had no help from Margaret, and he had just learnt that Louis XI had signed a truce with Burgundy for three months, so that French support was uncertain. He decided to fight it out with Edward, preferably by taking him by surprise in London at Easter. But Edward moved his men out of London to meet Warwick on Easter Sunday, and the two armies met at Barnet on April 14. Both Sir John and John III were there, fighting on the Lancastrian side in the retinue of the earl of Oxford. The armies had taken up their positions in darkness, and instead of facing each other in regular order, the right flank of each army was unopposed, and in the mist which covered the battlefield it was impossible to carry out the necessary manoeuvres to bring the armies into line. Oxford's men defeated the left hand battalion of Edward's army by a flank attack, and set off in pursuit. The rest of the line held, but swung through ninety degrees as the battle progressed, so that when Oxford's men were rallied and brought back into the battle, they were mistaken for the enemy by their own side, and attacked. They fled, crying treason, and at the same time the commander of Warwick's centre, Montagu was killed. Edward launched a renewed attack, and Warwick himself fled, only to be captured and killed a mile or so from the battlefield.

Sir John wrote immediately after the battle to reassure his mother:

'*Mother*, I commend myself to you and let you know, blessed be God, my brother John is alive and well, and in no danger of dying. Nevertheless he is badly hurt by an arrow in his right arm below the elbow, and I have sent a surgeon to him, who has dressed the wound; and he tells me that he hopes he will be healed within a very short time. John Mylsent is dead. God have mercy on his soul; William Mylsent is alive and all his other servants seem to have escaped.

'As for me, I am in good heart, blessed be God, and in no danger of my life if it suits me, for I am at liberty if need be.

'My lord archbishop is in the Tower. Nevertheless, I trust to God that he will be all right. He has got a safeguard for both himself and me. We have been troubled all the same since he got it, but now I understand that he has got a pardon, and so we hope all is well.

'There were killed on the battlefield half a mile from Barnet, on Easter Day [Monday], the earl of Warwick, Marquis Montagu, Sir William Tyrell, Sir Louis John and various squires from our part of the world, Godmerston and Bothe. On King Edward's side, Lord Cromwell, Lord Saye, Sir Humphrey Bourchier from our county, who is greatly mourned here, and other people on both sides, over a thousand in all.

'As for other news, it is reported here that Queen Margaret and her son have indeed landed in the west country; and I think that tomorrow or the next day King Edward will leave here to meet her and drive her out again.

'Please remember me to my cousin Lomnor, and thank him for his good will towards me if I had needed it, as I gathered from the bearer of this. Please tell him on my behalf that he should be very careful what he does or says as yet, for the world is very unstable as yet, as you will know within a month. The people here are very afraid, God has showed himself in a marvellous way, as Creator of All who can undo the world again when it pleases him: and I think in all likelihood he will show himself as marvellously again within a short while, and perhaps more than once in such cases.

'My brother has no money with him: I have helped him as much as I can, and more, so please remember him, for I cannot provide as well for myself.

'Written at London the Thursday in Easter Week. I hope to see you soon. Keep this note secret.

'Do not fear the ways things are going, for I trust that all will be well. If things continue as they are, I am not ruined, nor any of us, and if otherwise the same is true.'

By April 30, John III was well enough to write to his mother himself, though he complained that his treatment had cost £5 in a fortnight, and he had not a penny left. Unlike his brother, he had not yet got a pardon, so he signed his letter 'John of Geldeston', using the old medieval style of naming someone after the place where they were born, and wrote no address on the outside of the letter.

As Sir John had anticipated, God's marvels were not yet at an end. Perhaps the result was not what he had hoped: the earl of Oxford, now a fugitive in the north, was the best patron he had ever had, and a Lancastrian revival offered better chances than the return of the Yorkists. Queen Margaret and her son Prince Edward had indeed landed in the west country on April 14, the same day that the battle of Barnet was fought. The Lancastrian lords of the south-west, the duke of Somerset and earl of Devon, joined her there, and the army marched north to try to join their Welsh supporters under Jasper Tudor. Edward, by moving swiftly, succeeded in catching up with the Lancastrians near Tewkesbury, just before they could cross the Severn; and once again his luck held. The Lancastrian right abandoned a strong defensive position in order to attack the Yorkist vanguard and were routed; after a hard-fought battle, the Lancastrian centre and left in turn broke and fled. Prince Edward and many Lancastrian lords were killed; Queen Margaret was captured at Little Malvern

Priory. A list of those killed was sent to the Pastons not long afterwards, and copied out by James Gloys, Margaret's chaplain. The list begins 'Dead on the field', but there is then a list of eighteen names entitled 'These are the men who were beheaded', beginning with the duke of Somerset. Gloy's information was not entirely reliable, for he later marked two of the second list 'still alive'. Edward returned in triumph to London, where he found that his brother Richard duke of Gloucester had repelled an attack on the capital by the Bastard of Fauconberg and Kentish troops. On May 21, the last of the executions was carried out: Henry VI was killed in the Tower on Edward's order, and the Lancastrian cause seemed extinct.

The summer was an anxious one for the Pastons, despite Sir John's optimism. John III had to get his pardon, which took a little time, but on July 22 he was able to write to his mother:

'You will be pleased to know that this Wednesday Sir Thomas Wingfield sent a message to me that the king had signed my bill of pardon, which the said Sir Thomas delivered to me; and so by Friday at the latest I hope to have my pardon sealed by the chancellor.'

However, other affairs did not go so well. The duke of Norfolk was back in favour, and Caister had to be surrendered once more; in September Sir John wrote of its being back in the duke's hands, though we do not know when it was lost. He was nonetheless hopeful that it might be retrieved by negotiation, though he was always an optimist in such matters. He wrote to his brother on September 15:

'I would like to know if you have spoken to my lady of Norfolk or not, and what the attitude of her and her household is towards me and you, and whether it will be possible to get Caister back and get into their favour. Please find out what men are at Caister and under whose orders they are and get a spy who can go in and out; that way you will know their secrets. . .

'Please send me word if any of our friends or well-wishers are dead, for I fear that there is great mortality in Norwich and in other boroughs and towns in Norfolk: I assure you that it is the most widespread plague I ever knew of in England, for by my faith I cannot hear of pilgrims going through the country nor of any other man who rides or goes anywhere, that any town or borough in England is free from the sickness. May God put an end to it, when it please him. So, for God's sake, get my mother to take care of my younger brothers and see that they are not anywhere where the sickness is prevalent, and that they do not amuse themselves with other young people who go where the sickness is. If anyone has died of the sickness, or is infected with it, in Norwich, for God's sake let her send them to some friend of hers in the country; I would advise you to do the same. I would rather my mother moved her household into the country. . .'

Sir John had hopes of regaining favour at court through his engagement to Anne Haute, though he was very uncertain about the affair:

'I almost spoke with Mistress Anne Haute, but I did not. Nevertheless, in the next month or two I hope to get things settled one way or the other. She has agreed to talk to me, and hopes to offer me some relief, as she says. Please send me word how you are doing with my lady Elizabeth Bourchier; you have annoyed her in some way, but I cannot tell how. Send me word whether your hopes are better or worse.'

A fortnight later he asked John III to come to London by October 10, because he wanted his advice about various matters, including 'a final settlement to be made with Mistress Anne Haute', while John III still needed to get his pardon in its final form. At the end of October, John III wrote to his mother:

'As for Mistress Anne Haute, the business is being pursued by various of the queen's council, particularly by R. Haute; but he wants us to put forward proposals first, and we want them to put them first. Our affairs should go all the better for it.'

A new and unexpected crisis arose in November: Margaret Paston had been complaining of shortage of money for some time, but now she was forced with a demand which she was quite unable to meet, and wrote to John III:

'This is to let you know that my cousin Clere has sent to me for 160 marks which I borrowed from her for your brother. It happens that a friend of hers has recently lost more than three hundred marks and she had nothing she could get in cash, and so sent to me for the said hundred marks. And I do not know what to do for it, for in truth I have nothing to hand, and cannot get it, even if I should have to go to prison for it. So please talk to your brother and let me know what he will do about it quickly otherwise I will have to sell all my wood, and that would lose him more than two hundred marks if I die, and if I had to sell them now, no one would give within a hundred marks of their true value, because there are so many sales of wood in Norfolk at this time. So get him to arrange for the money quickly, if he wants my good will and if he wants to save the said woods for him to better avail in the future. Please send an answer quickly for my sake: I shall not be at ease until the matter is settled, for she has a bond of a hundred pounds for this, and it is no secret – many people know about it, and it seems a great shame to me that I parted with so much to your brother that I kept nothing back to pay the debts I have incurred for him; and many people who have learnt about it lately have said as much to me. And when I think of it, it grieves me keenly, considering that he never helped me over it, nor will ever try to repay any of the money he has had. . .

'As for news, my cousin Berney of Witchingham, Veyl's wife, London's wife and Picard of Tombland have passed to God; God have their souls. All this household and parish are safe, blessed be God. We live in fear, but we do not know where to flee that would be better than we are here. I am sending you five shillings to buy sugar and dates for me. I would like three or four pounds of sugar, and the rest in dates, and send me word what price per pound pepper, cloves, mace, ginger, cinnamon, almonds, rice, corinth raisins, galingale, saffron, grains and comfits are – let me know the price per pound of each and if they are cheaper in London than here I will send you money to buy such stuff as I want to have.'

Sir John's reply was not to Margaret's liking: not only did he refuse to make any arrangements to repay his mother, but he hinted that the reason she was writing as she did was due to the influence of her chaplain, James Gloys, who was her business adviser, and increasingly powerful within the household. Writing to John III at the end of November, she brought up the old matter of her husband's gravestone, which was still not made, though Sir John had asked for measurements to be taken in the church in September. She continued:

'I think from your brother's behaviour that he is tired of writing to me, and so I will not bother him by writing to him. You can tell him what is in my letters to you.'

Nonetheless, she was just as concerned about him as ever. On December 7 she wrote to John III:

'. . . Please send me word how your brother is. It was said here that he was dead, which made many people as well as me very sad. I was also told today that you were hurt in an attack made on you by thugs in disguise. At all events please send me word quickly how both you and your brother are, for I will not be at ease until I know. For the love of God, let both you and your brother beware where you go and with what companions you eat and drink, and in what places; for it was said openly here that your brother was poisoned.

'This week someone from Drayton was with me, and told me that various tenants there were saying that they did not know what they would do if your brother came home, and one of the duke of Suffolk's men was near and told them not to fear, because his journey would be cut short if he came there. So be careful of yourself, for I do not think they care what they do in order to be avenged and to turn you from your purpose, so that they can do what they want with Sir John Fastolf's lands. Think what great sorrow it would be to me if anything [happened to either of you]. I had rather you had never heard of his lands. Remember it was the destruction of your father. Do not trust too much in lords' promises nowadays to be surer of men's favour; there was a man, a lord's son himself, who quoted the example of Sir Robert Harcourt, who had the lords' favour after they came back to power, yet a little while afterwards their men killed him in his own house. A man's death is thought little of nowadays. Beware of deceit, for those who want things to go badly for you will speak to you in the most friendly way. . .'

Relations between the brothers – including Edmund II, who was now back at home – and their mother continued to grow worse during the following year. Sir John, short of money as ever, decided to sell the wood at Sporle, which produced a renewed outburst from his mother, who could scarcely believe her ears:

'If this were known, both your enemies and your friends would think you did it because you were desperately in need, or else that you were a waster and would waste your estates. If you had done it out of Sir John Fastolf's estates, people might have thought you did it as a matter of policy, because they are in such an uncertain state, and that you were getting what you could while it was in your possession to pay the debts incurred from it, but to do this on your estates will make men think you do it out of pure need. It is so near your enemies here that it will do you all the more harm, and make your friends more ashamed. If you behave like this you will make them all sure of what they have been doubtful about before, and make them plot all the more viciously against you. So, to avoid the great shame and inconvenience that may come of it, I require you, and moreover charge you on pain of losing my blessing, and as you want my good will, that if any such sale or bargain has been made, with or without your agreement, by Calle, or anyone else in your name, you must go back on it; for I would not for a thousand marks wish it to be understood that you had decided to act like this, nor that you had fallen into such need that you had to do so, for everyone would think it was through your own mismanagement. . . . If I learn that this is what you propose to do, you will be worse off by two hundred marks from my estates if I live for two years.'

The sale nonetheless went ahead; negotiations were in hand in February and John Osbern began the work of valuing timber in May. In October Richard Calle was busy selling timber and the sales went on piecemeal until 1475, despite Margaret's opposition.

As for James Gloys, the trouble between him and the brothers first comes into the open in a letter from Edmund II to John III in May:

'*Sir*, I commend myself to you. This is to let you know that my mother has made me dismiss Gregory from my service. He happened to be feeling randy – in plain terms he wanted a girl – and he had her in the rabbit warren yard. He was seen by two ploughmen of my mother's, who were as keen as he was, and asked him if they could join in; and faced with this request he did not say no, so that the ploughmen had her all night in a stable and she was out of Gregory's hands. He swears that he had nothing to do with her at my mother's place. All the same, my mother thinks he was at the bottom of the whole business, so the only remedy is to send him away. The last time you were here you asked me to have him if he left me, I am writing to tell you the real reason for his departure, according to my mother. But I am certain that the opposite is true – it is only that he cannot please everyone, but that gentleman [i.e. Gloys] is lord of his world. He has said he would remove anyone he wanted, and as you remember he removed someone fourteen miles in a morning; and now he has removed him I do not know how far unless you will show him better favour. Unless between us we give him a hand, I pray to God that we never prosper as he intends us to. So I ask you if you will agree to have him that you will be a better master to him for my sake, for I am as sorry to part with him as ever anyone alive was to part with his servant; and in truth, as far as I know, he is as faithful as anyone alive. I hope that my luck will be better than to live the whole time here in this fashion, but if I were out of this place, I assure you I would not change him for anyone I know. He is useful at various things, as you know.

'There has been a great row between Calle and me, which I will tell you about when I come, which will be next Wednesday, by the grace of God, who preserve you. Written at Mautby on Whitsun Eve.'

Edmund Paston

In July it was John III's turn to be in trouble; he wrote to Sir John of 'the proud, peevish priest James; who is ill-disposed to all of us', and described life in his mother's household in Norwich in bitter terms:

'She intends to go to the country and stay there again. Many quarrels are picked to get my brother E. and me out of her house. We do not easily get to bed without a scolding. Everything we do is badly done, and everything that James and Pekok do is well done. James and I are at loggerheads. We quarrelled in front of my mother calling each other 'proud priest' and 'proud squire'; my mother sided with him, so I have almost fouled the nest as far as my mother's house is concerned. Yet it will be the end of summer before I get myself a master.

'My mother intends in the near future to draw up a list of all her lands, and to make her will on the basis of the list: part will be given to my younger brothers for the term of their lives, with the reversion to you, part as my sister Anne's dowry with £100 has been paid, part to build the aisle for her at Mautby, part for a priest to sing for her and my father and their ancestors. And with this anger between James and me she has promised that I shall have nothing. God speed the plough! Indeed, you must arrange for my brother E. to go over [to Calais] with you, as he is undone. He will bring 20 nobles in his purse. My mother will not give nor lend either of you a penny in future.'

John III was still at home in October, despite his hopes of finding employment elsewhere, and the situation was not much better:

'James is always getting at me when my mother is there, choosing his words to irritate me and also to make my mother angry with me; as if to say that he wanted me to know that he does not care a fig for the best of us. And when he is rudest to me, I smile a little and tell him it is nice to hear these old stories. James is parson of Stokesby through J. Berney's gift. I think he is all the prouder for it.'

Meanwhile, Sir John was still doing his best to get back into favour at court, and to win over the duke and duchess of Norfolk. His relations with Anne Haute were still very ambivalent; reading between the lines, he was perhaps anxious not to offend someone so well connected, but had equally obviously no desire to marry her, though this may have been because he was no longer in a position to raise the necessary marriage settlement. In February he wrote to John III:

'As for news, I have spoken with Mistress Anne Haute at leisure and, blessed be God, we are as far as we were before, and I hope we will continue like that. I promised her that when I next had time to do so I would come to see her again, which will take some time, I think. Having done this ceremony once, I do not intend to tempt God again in this way.'

As far as the duke and duchess of Norfolk were concerned, the brothers thought that they saw an opportunity to press for the restoration of Caister when the ducal household gathered at Framlingham for the birth of the duchess's child in the late autumn. The progress of her pregnancy was eagerly reported, from the first news in June that she was expecting a child onwards: the Pastons, who had long ago been intimate members of the household, still had good friends there and were able to keep in touch with what was going on. They badly needed to recover Caister, because not only were things still going against them elsewhere, but the duke's possession of Caister, was likely to make trouble for Margaret's plans to live at Mautby, within sight of the castle, as she wrote in June:

'I am told that Harry Heydon has bought from the said lord [Bishop Wainfleet] both Saxthorpe and Titchwell, and has taken possession. We beat the bushes, and bear the loss and the shame, and other men get the birds. My lord is badly and foolishly advised about it. I am told Guton is likely to go the same way very soon; and as for Hellesdon and Drayton, I do not think things will change. What will happen to the rest, God knows I expect it will be as bad, or worse. We have only the losses. That ought to be remembered, and those who are at fault should feel guilty about it. And I was told lately that it is said privately by the people at Caister that I am likely to get little out of Mautby if the duke of Norfolk is still in possession at Caister; if we lose that, we lose the fairest flower of our garland. So see that he is soon out of possession, by my advice, whatever happens afterwards.'

In September, John III had made one very serious attempt to get the matter of Caister settled, and had a fairly good idea of how things stood in the duke's household. His report to Sir John was encouraging in some respects, even if the answer was still negative:

'*Sir*, I have been twice at Framlingham since you left, but the time the council was there, I saw your letter, which was more than well put. R.T. was not at Framlingham when the council was there, but I followed my own idea and delivered it to the council, and put the case as well, as best I could; my words were well received, but your letter a thousand times better. When they had read it, they showed it to my lady. After my lady had seen it I spoke to my lady, offering your service to my lord and her, and also offered that you would please my lord, and her even more, if you could agree, but without naming a sum. She would not interfere in the business but referred me back to the council, saying that if she said anything before my lord and the council had agreed, they would put the blame for it on her, which would be to her shame; but she promised to help if the council proposed it first. So I went back to the council and offered your service to my lord and a gratuity of £40 for having your place and lands at Caister back again, not mentioning your stuff or anything else. So they answered that your offer was more than reasonable, and if it was in their hands they knew what their conscience would lead them to do. They said they would propose it to my lord and so they did; but then the tempest arose, and he gave them such an answer that none of them would tell me what it was. But when I asked for an answer from them, they said that if some lords or great men proposed it to my lord the matter was yours. . .

'Do not reveal this, but in my opinion, if my lord chamberlain would send my lady a letter with some private token, and would also propose it to my lord of Norfolk when he comes to the parliament, Caister is certainly yours.'

Sir John tried to do his part when he met the duchess of Norfolk at Yarmouth in September or October, but his style of flattery seems to have misfired, expert courtier though he was.

On November 4 he wrote anxiously to his brother:

'Please find out my lady of Norfolk's attitude to me, and whether she was annoyed by what I said, or mocked or disdained it, when I spoke to her at Yarmouth between the place where I met her and her lodgings. For both my lady Brandon and Sir William asked me what I said to her then. They said that my lady said that I mocked her, and that I was supposed to have said that my lady was worthy of having a lord's son in her belly, because she would cherish it and look after it carefully. Indeed, I said that or something like it, and meant what I said. They imply that I said that she was taking things easy. I said that my lady was well built, with broad hips, so that I hoped she would bear a fine

179

child; he was not laced or braced in to his discomfort, but she had left him room to play in. They said that I said my lady was very large, and the child would have room enough to get out. So whether my lady is mocking me, or they are, I do not know, I meant well, in truth. . .'

At the end of November, Sir John obtained letters from the king to the duke, and he continued to try to get private messages to the duchess through one of her attendants, Jane Rothon, to whom he gave a diamond ring. On the other hand, he did not think that it was suitable for John to attend the confinement:

'If you think it right, I think that although neither Slyfield nor you, brother John, can come into my lady's chamber, yet my mother, if she was at Norwich, could speak to her, because she is a woman and of good reputation. I think there must be someone there with authority to make an agreement for me, or who knows my intentions; otherwise they will put things off, saying that they were prepared to speak to me at the king's request, but I was not there. So rather than fail, I will come home at once if I hear from you. Slyfield has agreed to wait for a week for my sake to get the business settled. Please make him welcome, and if he has to wait, I must remember his expenses. If I am sent for and he waits at Norwich in the meanwhile, it would be best to put his horse at the Maid's Head, and I will pay their bill.'

But all that came of these efforts, and of an interview between Bishop Wainfleet and the duchess at the child's christening on December 18, was a promise that the duke would meet the bishop of Winchester to discuss the matter in the spring. Wainfleet had an interest in seeing Caister restored to Sir John, since this was in effect his part of the bargain over the settlement of Sir John's will. Whether the interview took place, we do not know: at all events the duke continued to hold Caister.

Sir John and his brother now took service with the garrison at Calais, possibly as a means of earning money, but equally probably out of boredom with the weary life they led in England. Sir John made arrangements for his brother to join the garrison in November 1472, and he himself went there the following January. At the end of the month he went down to Ghent, to see the duke of Burgundy and meet some old acquaintances from his journey there in 1468.

He wrote to John III on February 3:

'As for news, there is little here except that the duke of Burgundy and my lady his wife are well: I was with them last Thursday at Ghent. Peter Metteney is well and Mistress Gretkyn too, and Babekyn asks to be remembered to you. She has been very ill, but it has done her good, for she is prettier and slimmer than she was. She did not welcome me; all I got was "How is master John your brother?" so I was cross and said something jealous, because I did not like her caring so much for you when I was present.'

He was back in England in early April, and came and went between England and Calais during the summer; Edmund, too, was there, in July, but despite the arrangement made in November, it does not seem that John went over during 1473; as always, it was he who was left to manage the family affairs in Norfolk. Sir John had great difficulty in getting enough men to go over with him. In April, he told John:

'. . . I have been and still am troubled by my over-generous and gentle handling of my servants and their unkindness in return. Plattyng, your man, today asked to take his leave of me tomorrow at Dover, even though Thryston, your other man, has left me and John Myryell and W. Woode, who promised you and Daubeney, God have his soul, at Caister that if you would take him in to serve me again he would never leave me; and on the strength of that I have kept him for three years to play St George and Robin Hood and the sheriff of Nottingham* and now when I want good horses he has gone into Barnesdale,† and I have no horse-keeper. . .

'Most of the soldiers who went over with Sir Robert Green have got leave and are coming home; the highway is full. My carriage was two hours further behind me that I thought. I thought that I was in for a real Good Friday fast and all my gowns and splendid things had been lost; but everything was safe.'

* In Christmas plays?
† The forest associated with Robin Hood in early sources.

Early in June, he was about to embark again but had only three men with him, two of whom were threatening to leave, so he asked John III to send up to four men across to him. He added:

'Please send me a new vestment of white damask for a deacon which is with my other stuff at Norwich. . . . I want to make an arming doublet out of it, even if I have to give a velvet gown to get another vestment some other time; send it as quickly as you can to Hoxon to send me. I hoped to have a good time at Calais this Whitsuntide, and am well prepared and equipped, except that these people keep letting me down; there is good material for a story in it. Some men would have hurried to Calais though they had nothing better to do, and some think it wise and useful to be there now, well out of the way.

'As for the bishop and I, we are nearer to agreement than we were, so my share is now all the lands at Flegg, Hellesdon manor, Tolthorpe and tenements in Norwich and Earlham except Fairchild's, but fare-well Drayton, the devil pay them for it!'

Sir John's pleasures at Calais seem to have included his usual flirta-tions. Writing to Edmund in July, he gives instructions for the delivery of a present:

'I am sending a pretty little box with this which I would like Juddy to deliver to the woman he knows of and ask her to take it to the man she knows of; that is telling you as much as you all know well enough, but do not let it be known that you know.

'Please send word as you used to of how she is, and whether I am out of favour and someone else in, or not, and whether she will leave Calais as soon as you say she will, or not. By God, I would gladly be with you, and will soon be there, with God's grace.

'As for my brother John, I hope to see him in Calais, within the month, he will probably take ship tomorrow or the next day at Yar-mouth, and go to Santagio de Compostela [on pilgrimage], and he writes that he will come home by Calais.'

There was a more serious side to Sir John's presence in Calais. War with France was becoming a distinct possibility, and in August Sir John was negotiating with a well-known armourer at Bruges for a complete suit of armour, while the letter to Edmund contained careful instructions about his weapons. In September Lord Hastings thanked him for his assistance to his deputy as governor of Calais. But Edward's plans for taking his revenge on Louis were held in abeyance by the fact that the duke of Burgundy was preoccupied elsewhere.

At home, Margaret was as much under the influence of James Gloys as ever. In January she had written to him with long instructions, among them rules for the education of Walter, her youngest and favourite son. Nonetheless, in July, Sir John tried to make peace with her, protesting that it was a long while since he had heard from her, and that his latest misdemeanor, an attempt to mortgage the manor at Sporle was something he had been forced to do by lack of money from her. He was able to report one piece of good news, that he had at last obtained probate of his father's will, and was beginning to deal with the estate. In the end Margaret lent him £100 to buy off the proposed mortgage at Sporle which he did at the end of 1474. At some time during October 1473, James Gloys died, and Margaret decided to move back to Norwich for the moment: Sir John, on hearing the news, could not refrain from commenting to his brother.

'... I am very glad that she will now act according to your advice. Beware from now on that no such fellow creeps between her and you. If you take a little trouble you could live very well if she pleased. You might as well ride with two horsemen at her expense as James or Richard Calle.'

A full reconciliation seems to have taken place at the end of the year, since Sir John's letters to his mother in 1474 are much friendlier. On 20 February he wrote:

'*Right honourable and most tender and good mother*, I commend myself to you, begging you for your blessing each day, which I hope I have. I thank you for the kindness and welcome which I had, and the great expense which you went to, when I was last with you; may God give me grace to deserve after this. I think it is a long time since I heard from you or from Pekok your servant with information about how he has done in selling barley from my rents. If he has not answered by the time this note reaches you, please send him and the money here quickly; if I had not been waiting for it, I think I would have been at Calais by now. For the French king is said to be at Amiens with a great army, only sixty miles from Calais, and if he or his men rode to Calais and I was not there, I would be sorry.'

During the autumn of 1474, Sir John was ill, as were his brother Edmund and his grandmother; he went home to recuperate, and in November had recovered. He told Margaret:

'Your care has made me completely better, for which I thank God and you; indeed, I was afraid that I would have perished on the way to you from weakness, being only just recovered from my illness. But, God thank you, I had such an appetite while I was with you that I felt on the way back that God and you had made me stronger than I think I was before, and each day I felt better than before.'

He was not completely better, however; at the end of the month he was still complaining of pains in his heel, and there was evidently more sickness about, since Margaret advised him to leave London as soon as possible. Edmund and his grandmother recovered, but his uncle William's daughter died about the same time.

In January 1475 Margaret wrote to ask Sir John whether he was fully recovered:

'I thank you for the flagons you sent me: they are very good and I am very pleased with them. I will be as good a housewife for you as I can and I would be for myself. Send me word how your sickness is that you had in your eye and your legs and if God will not let you have health, thank him and bear it patiently, and come back home to me, and we will live as God will give us grace to do.'

Sir John replied that he was almost better, but the following September he had a recurrence of some kind of sickness, which he blamed on the air at Calais. His health seems to have remained indifferent from now on. John III, who was usually healthy, was also ill at Calais at the same time, but attributed it to cold. In October he was still recovering, and was wearing as many 'coats, hose and boots' as he could in order to get better quickly.

The years from 1474 onwards see a considerable drop in the surviving correspondence, partly because the Pastons' affairs were less complex, partly through the chance survival of letters, and partly because with John III often in Norfolk managing affairs there was less need for business notes. Such letters as do survive are often about marriages. Sir John's longstanding engagement to Anne Haute was slowly coming to an end. In November 1473, he was making enquiries about the possibility of a release from any contract that might exist, which would need dispensation from Rome:

'You asked me also to send you news of how I was getting on in my affairs, especially with Mistress Anne Haute. I have had an answer back from Rome that the well of grace and ointment sufficient for such a sore is to be found there, and I may be dispensed with. Nonetheless, my proctor there is asking a fee of 1000 ducats, but Master Lacy, another Rome-runner here, who says he knows my proctor there as well as Bernard knew his shield, says he means only a hundred ducats or two hundred at most; so more will happen after this.'

After this, all we hear of her is two brief references: in February 1477 the business was discussed between Sir John, a cardinal and lord chamberlain, and in August Sir John hoped that the matter would be at an end that law-term, using it as an excuse for his lack of money.

It was in fact Sir John's sister Anne who was next of the family to marry. In 1472 negotiations were under way for her to marry the grandson of Sir William Yelverton, Sir John's old opponent in the law-courts. The match was not easily arranged: John III who was the first to mention it, in June 1472, only did so to say that his mother would not abandon Yelverton in favour of another suitor. A year and a half later, Sir John wrote:

'As for my sister Anne, I understand that she has been very ill, but I thought she was married by now. As for Yelverton, he said that he would have her if she had her money, and otherwise not; so I do not think things are very certain. But amongst everything else please beware that her old love for Pampyng is not renewed. He has now left me; I do not know what he will do.'

Sir John's fears that Anne might imitate the example of her sister Margery and marry a family servant were unfounded, but it was a long while before the marriage took place. In January 1476, Sir John thought he had found a better match for her, 'Skipwith's son and heir from Lincolnshire, worth five or six hundred marks a year'. In the end Anne married Yelverton in the spring of 1477.

John III, too, was in search of a wife; in March 1470 he had ended a letter to Sir John, half in jest, 'Please get us a wife somewhere, for "it is better to marry in the Lord than to burn".' In 1474 he was pursuing several possibilities, and in July seems to have been wooing two ladies at once, and perhaps making enquiries about another. He wrote to Sir John in London 'or to his brother Edmund in his absence' on July 25:

'*Right worshipful sir*, I commend myself to you. Please remember, before you leave London to speak to the wife of Harry Eberton, the draper, and to tell her that I have been offered a marriage in London worth 600 marks or more. I asked you to talk to her because I could not stay in London myself: but I make this reservation, that if Mrs Eberton will negotiate with me, do not make an agreement in the other place even if Eberton will not give as much with Miss Elizabeth his daughter as I would get with the other, because I have taken a liking to the said Miss Elizabeth Eberton. Please say to Eberton's wife that what I spoke to her about shall be increased rather than lessened on my side, and if she will negotiate with me I will be in London for that reason alone within a fortnight of this note, with God's grace, who preserve you and yours.

'Written at Norwich on St James's day.

'Also, sir, I beg you, as I requested, to talk to John Lee or his wife, or both of them, and find out how the thing at Blackfriars is going, and see or speak to the girl herself, and with her father and mother, before you leave; please ask John Lee's wife to send me a note how things are going and whether I need to come up to London quickly or not, or else abandon everything.'

From about the same time we have a note from John III to a possible bride, perhaps the girl at Blackfriars:

'Since I may not be there as often as I would like to deliver my own message, my own fair mistress Anne, please accept this note as my messenger to remember me to you most faithfully and to say that I above all other men wish to know that you are in good health, which I pray God increase as it most pleases you. And, mistress, although I have given you little cause to remember me for lack of acquaintance, yet please do not forget me when you count up your suitors, to be included in their numbers. I pray you, Mistress Anne, by the service that I owe you, please assure me as soon as you decently may of your intentions; your and my faithful friends John Lee and my mistress his wife promised both you and me at our first and last meeting that as soon as either of them know the intentions of you and your friends, they would send me word. If they do so, I hope to see you soon afterwards.

'And now farewell, my own fair lady, and God give you good rest, for I think you will be in bed. Written on my way home on St Mary Magdalene's day at midnight.

Your own John Paston

'Mistress Anne, I am proud that you can read English, so please get to know my clumsy hand: I hope you will get to know it better if I have my way. But when you have read this note, please burn it or keep it secret, as I trust you faithfully.'

By November, these affairs had faded, and Sir John was engaged in wooing Lady Walgrave on his brother's behalf, with the help of a friend of John III called Dawnson; meanwhile, John III was busy furthering Dawnson's suit with another lady. As Sir John said 'it would be a pity if such crafty wooers as you two should be successful unless you are really in love'. Lady Walgrave certainly was not; Sir John had a decidedly difficult interview with her, in which his best courtly manner failed to cut much ice, as he reported on December 11:

'... I have done my duty, and discovered my Lady Walgrave's attitude which, so God help me to be blunt with you, offers nothing which I could take as encouragement. She refuses to take your ring and keep it with her, even though I told her it would in no way commit her, but that I know from you of old that I was sure you would rather part with whatever you held dearest in the world so that it could be in her presence and remind her of you once a day: but she would not take it.

She did not want, as she said, to encourage you in any way by doing it, and she asked me not to take any more trouble over it, because she would keep to the answer she had given you before. She thought that both you and I would have been content to leave it at that if it had not been for what her sister Genevieve said.

'When I understood all this, and that overnight she told the person who was go-between between her and me to tell me to bring her muskball, then I asked her if she was angry with me because of it, and she said no. Then I told her that I had not sent it to you, for sin of my soul, and how I had written to you saying why I would not send it to you because I thought you would have slept the worse for it. But now I told her, God help me, that I would send it to you, and advise you not to put too much hope in her, because she was too hard-hearted a lady for a young man to trust in, which I thought you could not and would not do for all my words and advice. On the other hand, she is not angry, and did not forbid me to let you have her muskball to keep. So do what you like with it. I wish it had done some good. By God, I spoke so well for you that I could not do it again: so I am sending you your ring and the unlucky muskball as well. Make what you can of the business after this. I am unlucky in wooing, both for myself and other people.'

In 1475, plans for the long-awaited invasion of France came to a head. Due to a change of heart by Charles the Bold in Burgundy, who now had designs on the German empire and was less interested in his old quarrel with France, Edward launched his invasion with little help from abroad. Charles himself was fully occupied by the siege of Neuss, a town in the Rhineland belonging to the archbishop of Cologne, which had been going on since July 1474, and had become something of a *cause célèbre*. In January 1475, Sir John wrote to John III from Calais:

'Tomorrow I intend to ride into Flanders to get horses and armour, and I shall perhaps see the siege at Neuss before I return, if I have time; if I do so, it is likely to be a fortnight before I am back here. . . As for news here, there is little that is certain except that the siege of Neuss by the duke of Burgundy continues, and the emperor has besieged, not far from there, a castle and another town where the duke's men are in the same way. Also, the French king, men say, has come near the river Somme with 4000 spears and some men think that he will attack the duke's lands on the day the truce ends, if not before.'

Sir John's information was accurate: on May 1, Louis invaded Burgundy, and six weeks later Charles was forced to give up the siege of Neuss. Edward was not deterred, and early in July he disembarked an army of some 1100 men at Calais. Among the army were Sir John, John III and Edmund. Margaret was dubious about this. On May 23, after complaining about the war taxes – 'the king takes so much from us here, both from poor and rich, that I do not know how we shall live unless things improve' – she warns Sir John:

'... if your brothers go across the sea, advise them as you think best for their safety, for some of them are only young soldiers, and have little idea of what it means to be a soldier, and how to put up with what a soldier has to do. God save you all and send me good news of you all.'

The king waited at Calais for ten days, until Charles of Burgundy arrived on July 14, but instead of the army for which the English still hoped, he brought only a small bodyguard. Relations between the English and Burgundians quickly deteriorated; Charles would not admit them to any of his towns on their march south, and within a month Edward had decided to negotiate with Louis, despite the opposition of his brother, Richard of Gloucester, and a few other lords. Lord Hastings, Sir John's patron and commander of Calais, was in favour of negotiations, and he, Clarence and the earl of Northumberland helped to arrange the final terms at Picquigny on August 29. Although there was a certain amount of resentment at this inglorious end to the campaign, the treaty did bring commercial advantages for England and a substantial pension for Edward from Louis.

All three brothers seem to have returned home in September 1475 with the army; Sir John continued to spend some time in Calais for the next two years. In 1477, a boon companion of his, John Pympe, wrote to him to ask him to bring a good horse for him if he could find one, though he had other things to tease Sir John about:

'By Mary, we have heard it said that the *fraus* of Bruges with their tall caps have given some of you great blows, and that the way they bear arms is to strike at the mouth and the thick end of the thigh; but indeed we are not worried about you, for we know well that you are good enough at defence. But we hear it said that they are so bold that they give you more blows than you do them, and that they strike harder than you do. But I think that the English ladies and gentlewomen, and ordinary women too, can do as well as they and need not learn anything from them, so we are afraid lest their bold hearts move them to make war on you as well. But God save you from that, for you would have much to do then; it would be better and easier to labour for three or four days with pick and spade to level your sandhills, as we hear you are doing very very skilfully, than to stand up against their fierce attacks for one day and either win or save your reputation. Do not expect a rescue party from us, for God help me, we have enough to do in these parts with the same wars. . .'

For all his amusements, Sir John continued to pursue more serious matters, and had not lost hope of recovering Caister. His brothers and uncle agreed to press his claim while he was away in Calais, but as usual matters dragged on, influential lords made promises which they did not keep, meetings were arranged but failed to take place.

In September he reported to his mother:

'I had good hopes of getting Caister back. The king spoke to my lord of Norfolk about it, and it was very likely to have happened, but in the end it was put off to next law-term; by which time the king has ordered him to take his council's advice and to be sure that this title is good, or else the king has assured him that if he wants to stay in favour he must do me right and justice.'

That autumn, he drew up a petition to the king, and was evidently in contact with the duke, for in January 1476 he was at Framlingham. On January 17, he wrote in haste to his mother:

'This is to let you know that – not at the best time for me – it so happens that my lord of Norfolk, who was in good health yesterday, died to-night about midnight; so all who loved him must now do whatever may be to his honour and the good of his soul. In this part of the world, there is not much cloth of gold to be had for the covering of his body and hearse, so, as everyone is doing his best to help, I encouraged my lord's council by telling them that I hoped to get one for that day as long as it had not been cut up or put to other use. So please send me word if you can get hold of the woven cloth I bought for my father's tomb; I undertake that it will be returned safely and undamaged at my expense. I hope to get thanks for this, and great assistance in the future. Either Symme or Mother Brown can deliver it to me tomorrow by seven o'clock.

'As for other things, I have sent my servant Richard Tornor to London, who I hope will bring back good news, and I hope to see you within four days. Written on Wednesday the seventeenth day of January, in the fifteenth year of King Edward.'

John Paston K.

What Sir John did not say, writing as he was from Framlingham itself, was that he was also sending a message to Caister immediately to claim possession of it. For once he had done the right thing, though John III warned him on January 23 that his swift action had aroused criticism:

'. . . For I assure you that your sending a messenger to Caister is taken badly among my lord's people, so much so that some say you cared little for my lord's death if you made entry of his lands so soon after he died without the agreement of his council. It is thought by those who are your friends in my lord's household that, if my lady can once get a grant of wardship of the child, she will occupy Caister along with the other lands and lay the blame on your unkind haste to make entry without her assent. So at all costs get a patent sealed by the king before her, if you possibly can.'

Sir John replied at once, defending his action, and saying that if he had known the duke was going to die, he would have seized the place before he died; moreover, there was general agreement that his action was justified, even among the duke's council. The duke had been unreasonable to him, and they felt he was right to do it, whatever allegiance he owed to the duke. John III was still worried that his brother would press his luck too far, but there were rumours that Sir John intended to seize the place. He did his best to allay such fears: on February 3 he wrote:

'Robert Brandon and John Colville have managed to tell my lady that you wanted to get Caister from her by force during this frost, while the moat is frozen. She intended to send R. Brandon and others to keep the place until such time she had asked me whether that was your intention. I advised her to let R. Brandon to stay at Norwich at his own expense rather than at the tavern at Yarmouth at her expense; for I let her know that you do not intend to enter the place except with her assent and knowledge, as I well know.'

At the beginning of May, however, when Sir John returned from a journey to Calais, such ideas were still being mooted, and John III wrote, using a false name for Caister:

'As for the castle of Sheene, there is no one in it except Colin and his wife, and a goose could get it. But I do not like that method, and my mother agrees. Do not use it if there is any other way.'

Sir John did take the 'other way', and at the end of the month he was able to report success:

'As for my affairs, unless they get worse, they are going as well as I could wish, blessed be God, except that it will cost me much money, and has cost me much labour. The king must have 100 marks, and other costs will come to 40 marks. My case has been examined by the king's council and declared before all the lords, and now lacks nothing but privy seals and writing to Master Colville to quit. The king has promised me everything I want him to do, and all the lords, judges and sergeants have affirmed that my title is good...'

Two short sentences in a letter to John III at the end of June mark the conclusion of the long battle for possession:

'Blessed be God, I have Caister as I want it,
God hold it better than it has been held before.'

If Sir John's affairs prospered, John III's were less successful. Sir John had been trying to find a patron for him, proposing Lord Fitzwalter, who lived at Attleborough and was also a member of Calais garrison; some kind of arrangement may have been made since John III spoke of him in later years as 'my master'. He was still looking for a wife, asking Sir John to find him 'an old thrifty draught-wife from London', and also sounding out a possible match with Fitzwalter's sister-in-law. Serious negotiations with an unknown lady were in progress during the summer, but came to nothing. Otherwise all we hear of him at this time is that he had a feverish illness at the end of August, vividly portrayed by Sir John in a letter to his mother:

'This is to let you know that on Tuesday, the day I left you. I was with my brother John at Attleborough by eight o'clock in the evening, and found him in such a state then that if you had seen him you would be as glad to have him now as a new son. I did not think he would have lived until morning; indeed, I dare say that if we had not happened to come to him, he would not have been alive on Wednesday; for since Saturday he has slept less than four hours, three of which since I arrived, until tonight. Tonight, blessed be God, he has slept well and with God's grace I am sure he will be all right, for his fever has gone and everything that lay in his stomach and side is getting better. Within a day or two, I hope he will be so strong that I can leave him, and he hopes to see you within a few days, or so he says.

'On Wednesday I said to him that I wished that he and I were at Norwich; he worried about this all night and because he did not sleep as well as he might have, he decided to come to Norwich, and in a fit of temper he insisted on riding off – he did not want a horse-litter, he was so strong. Nonetheless, we did not think he could ride a mile, and did not think it would be possible to get beyond Wymondham. When he was mounted, for all that we said, he rode so well that he led us a dance, going faster than we could easily follow him. He was at Wymondham, indeed, in at least a quarter of an hour less than an hour, and rested there for an hour. He mounted again, and was here in less than an hour and a half. And now he says he is sure to sleep well, because he says he has never failed to sleep well in the bed he has chosen at Frensh's; so I hope he is safe.'

John III's luck changed at last for the better early in 1477. Although Sir John was still keeping a lookout for prospective brides in London, he found a match in Norfolk, and a love-match at that. One of the first letters we have about it is dated February 9. It comes from the mother of the girl in question, Dame Elizabeth Brews, wife of Sir Thomas Brews of Topcroft, who lived some fifteen miles south of Norwich. Clearly the negotiations were already well advanced by this stage:

'*Cousin*, I commend myself to you, thanking you for the great welcome that you gave me and all my people last time I was at Norwich. And you promised that you would never break the business to Margery until you and I were agreed. But you have made her such an advocate for you that I get no rest by day or night because she is always calling on me and urging me to bring the business into effect.

'And, cousin, Friday is St Valentine's day, when every bird chooses itself a mate; if you would like to come on Thursday night and arrange to stay till Monday, I trust to God you will speak to my husband, and I shall pray that we shall bring the matter to a conclusion. For, cousin, it is a poor oak that is cut down at the first stroke; for you will be reasonable, I trust to God, who have you ever in his merciful keeping.'

> *By your cousin Dame Elizabeth Brews, who shall*
> *be called otherwise by God's grace*

Thomas Kela, the family chaplain, who wrote this note for Elizabeth Brews, also sent a letter of his own, encouraging John III in his suit, and a little later he wrote out two letters to John III from Margery herself:

'*Right reverend and worshipful and my very well-beloved Valentine*, I commend myself to you with all my heart, wishing to hear that all is well with you: I beseech Almighty God to keep you well according to his pleasure and your heart's desire. If you would like to know how I am, I am not well in body or heart, nor shall be until I hear from you.

> *For no creature knows what pain I endure*
> *On pain of death, I dare not reveal it.*

'My lady my mother has put the matter very diligently to my father, but she can get no more than you know of, which God knows, I am very sorry about.

'But if you love me, as I hope indeed that you do, you will not leave me because of it; if you did not have half the estates you have, I would not forsake you, even if I had to work as hard as any woman alive.

And if you command me to keep me true wherever I go
Indeed I will do all I can to love you, and nothing more.
And if my friends say I do wrong, they shall not stop me from doing it.
My heart bids me to love you for ever
Truly, over anything on earth.
However angry they are, I hope it will be better in future.

'No more for now, but the Holy Trinity have you in keeping. Please do not let any creature on earth see this note, but only you. And this letter was written at Topcroft with a very sad heart.'

By your own M.B.

'*Right worshipful and well-beloved Valentine*, I commend myself to you in my most humble fashion, I thank you with all my heart for the letter you sent me by John Bykerton, from which I understand that you intend to come to Topcroft in a short time, and with no other errand or business than to bring to a conclusion the business between my father and you. I would be the happiest creature alive if the business could take effect. And because you say that if you come and find matters no further on than before, you do not want to put my father and my lady my mother to any more expense or trouble for that reason for a good while afterwards, my heart is very heavy; and if you come, and nothing can be settled, then I shall be even sadder and full of sorrow.

'As for myself, I have done what I can or may, God knows. I must tell you plainly that my father will part with no more money over it than £100 and 50 marks, which is a long way from fulfilling your wishes. So if you could be content with that and my poor person, I would be the merriest maiden on earth. If you do not think that would satisfy you, or that you want much more wealth, as I understood from you before, good, true, and loving Valentine, do not trouble to come again about it, but let it pass, and not be spoken of again, and I will be your true lover and pray for you as long as I live. No more for now, but Almighty Jesus preserve you, both body and soul.'

By your Valentine Margery Brews

Margery's fears were well-founded: John III came over about the beginning of March, but on 8 March negotiations were at a standstill. Sir Thomas thought that John's estates were too small, but he himself could not afford to give a larger dowry, saying in a letter to Sir John he was loath 'to bestow so much on one daughter that the other sisters should be worse off'. He appealed to Sir John for help, asking him 'to put his good will and some of his money into the matter'. On the same day John III also wrote from the Brews' house at Topcroft to his mother, to arrange a meeting between Dame Elizabeth and her at Norwich. Writing to Sir John the next day, he said:

'. . . As for the business between myself and Margery Brews, I am still uncertain about it, because her father is so hard; but I think I have the goodwill of my lady her mother and her.'

Sir John, on his way to Calais, was writing on the same day:

'I have received your letter and your man J. Bykerton, through whom I knew all about the business with Mistress Brews, which, if it is as he says, I pray God bring it to a good end. . .

'Please send a letter to Calais about how you get on with Mistress Brews. Bykerton tells me she loves you well. I had rather, on pain of death, that you had her than Lady Walgrave, though she sings well to the harp. Clopton is afraid of Sir T. Greye, for he has lately become a widower, and men say that he knows her of old.'

As a result of the meeting between Margaret and Dame Elizabeth, Margaret agreed to give John III the manor of Sparham to add to his estates, and wrote to ask Sir John for his agreement. Sir John replied that he was sorry to hear of the difficulties over the marriage:

'I would be as glad as any man, and more content now that he should have her than any other girl he planned to marry – considering her person, her youth, and the family she comes from, the love on both sides, the high favour she is in with her father and mother, the kindness

of her father and mother in giving her a dowry, the good opinion they
have of my brother, the respectable and virtuous reputation of her
father and mother, all of which indicates that the girl should be virtuous and good. Considering all this, and the help that my brother
needs, I am not surprised that you have parted with the manor of
Sparham and given it to him. . .'

Sir John pointed out a problem: the manor was entailed and not held
in fee simple, and might thus revert to him or his children. He was
prepared to guarantee not to disturb his brother's possession of the
manor, but as executor of his father's will could not actually ratify the
gift. He wrote encouragingly to his brother a fortnight later, but when
it was suggested that Sparham should be exchanged for lands which
he held in fee simple, he was not pleased, and wrote sternly to his
brother that he should not hope to get things which his friends were
not in a position to give him. He went on:

'Your business is spoken of far and wide, and if it goes not better than
this I wish it had never been discussed. I am rumoured to be so obstinate that I am hindering everything. I do not think that things are
happy, or well handled or skilfully dealt with if they cannot be con-
cluded without inconvenience, and I would never agree to such a bargain. If I had started the business, I would have hoped for a better
conclusion, unless they are not serious. Things have been taken this far
without my advice; please finish it as well without my advice. If it
goes well, I shall be glad; if otherwise, it is a pity. Please do not bother
me any more about the business.'

Evidently negotiations broke down at this stage, for on June 11 Margaret wrote from Mautby to Dame Elizabeth to arrange a new meeting, saying

'I know you will remember all the negotiations at various times over
the marriage of my cousin Margery, your daughter, and my son John,
which I have been as glad about, and now lately as sorry about, as any
marriage in my life. Where and in whom the fault of the breach lies, I
cannot tell for certain, but, madam, if it lies with me or any of my
family, please assign a day when my cousin your husband and you

expect to be at Norwich on your way to Sall, and I will come there to meet you, and I think that before we part we will find out where the fault is and with your advice and help as well as mine, we shall find some way of preventing it from being broken off; for if it was, it would do no honour to either party, especially to those who are at fault, seeing that it has been so much talked about.'

Whether the meeting took place is not clear; at the end of June Elizabeth Brews was ill, and unable to talk to her husband about the marriage. Apparently he was going back on the original terms, and John III got his mother to write to Dame Elizabeth accordingly. Exactly how he won his bride we do not know, but with so much goodwill on both sides, the financial obstacles were overcome, and they were married during the summer, probably in August or September.

In January 1478 John III wrote to Sir John:

'And, sir, as for my housewife, I wanted to take her to see her father and friends now, for I think she will be out of fashion in the summer. And so on my way from my father-in-law's to Mautby, I took her on a visit to Master Playter, at whose house I wrote this note. . .'

With John III happily married and Sir John's engagement to Anne Haute still unresolved, the family now turned their attention to a match for Edmund II. Sir John had found a possible match for him in 1477; now it was John III who suggested a mercer's daughter from London in a letter to Margaret. As Edmund was staying with John III at his house at Swainsthorpe, at the time, he presumably approved of the idea, but nothing came of it. John ended his letter:

'Your daughter of Swainsthorpe and her guest E. Paston ask to be remembered to you in most humble fashion, beseeching you for your blessing. As for my brother Edmund of Swainsthorpe, for all the entreaties of his hostess your daughter and myself we could not keep him here, but he wanted to be at home with you at Mautby last Sunday night; and as he left here we heard from Frensh's wife, that, God forgive you, mother, you had given him leave to take his ease here with us for seven or eight days. And so the wretch lost our goodwill, but stayed all the same. Your daughter is sending you part of such stuff as

I was able to send her from London, asking you to take it in good part, although she is sending you little enough. But as for dates, I must say that you are getting at least two pounds less than were meant for you, for she thinks that dates are very much to her taste at the moment, whatever that means.'

The last remark was presumably a hint that Margery was expecting a child, as their son Christopher was born in August: Sir John wrote on August 25 to congratulate them on the arrival of 'my fair nephew Christopher', but complained gently that he had learnt the news from men coming from Norfolk on foot before John III had managed to send a messenger on horseback. Sir John was in London for most of this year; now that Caister was his, the long-standing battle over Hellesdon and Drayton was being renewed, against the duke of Suffolk, who now had possession of both. Sir John attempted to prevent the felling of woods at Drayton, and pressed his claim to Hellesdon. His agent Whitley reported in May:

'As for Hellesdon, my lord of Suffolk was there on Wednesday in Whitsun week, and dined there, and had one of the stewponds netted and took a great many fish. Yet he has left you a pike or two for when you come; that day will be a great encouragement to all your friends and will discourage your enemies. As for his behaviour when he was there, no one ever played Herod in the Corpus Christi Play★ better or more aptly than he did. It was afternoon and the weather was hot, and he was so weak with sickness that his legs would not support him, but two men had great difficulty to keep him on his feet. And judgement was passed on you. Some said "Kill him!" some said "Put him in prison!" And my lord came out and said he would meet you with a spear, and no other amends would do for the trouble you have given him but your heart's blood, and he will get it with his own hands; for if you have Hellesdon and Drayton you will have his life as well.'

Whitley also reported that Margaret Paston had been very ill, 'so ill that she thought she was going to die and has made her will. . . I do not know all the circumstances yet, so that is all I can put in writing, but I have been promised more information before I left.'

★ Herod was played as unreasonable and with a violent temper.

She evidently continued in ill-health because in May the following year Sir John was sending her 'Genoa treacle' from his apothecary, with careful instructions as to which of the three pots he was sending were most likely to be good. Margaret was also very anxious that something should at last be done about her husband's tomb at Bromholm, and in May 1478 gave Sir John the cloth of gold which had been lent for the duke of Norfolk's funeral, with instructions to sell it to raise money for the tomb:

'I greet you, and send you God's blessing and mine: this is to let you know that I have sent you by Whitley the cloth of gold, charging you that it is not to be sold for any other purpose but for the making of your father's tomb, as you promised me in writing. If you sell it for any other purpose, I swear I will never trust you so long as I live. Remember that it cost me twenty marks to redeem it from pledge, and if I were not glad to see the tomb made I would not part with it. Remember what expense I have had because of you lately, which will make things difficult for the next two years. When you are better off I hope you will remember it.

'My cousin Clere is spending over £100 at Bromholm on the choirstalls and elsewhere and Heydon likewise; if nothing is done for your father, it will be a great shame to us all, especially to see him lie as he does.'

At the end of 1478 and in the first half of 1479 we hear something about Margaret's two youngest sons, William and Walter. William was still at Eton, even though he was nearly twenty and taking a young man's interest in the young ladies of Eton. Writing to John III, he describes his fancy of the moment:

'As for the young gentlewoman, I will tell you how I first made her acquaintance. Her father is dead. There are two sisters; I was at the elder sister's wedding with my landlady, and was also invited by the bridegroom himself, called William Swanne, who lives at Eton. It happened that my landlady said more about me than I deserved, and her mother told her to make me welcome, as indeed she did. She does not live permanently where she is now; her home is in London, but her mother and she came to a place of hers five miles from Eton because it was near to the gentleman who married her other daughter. Next Monday, that is the first Monday in Lent proper, her mother and she will go to the pardon at Sheen and so to London, to stay at a place of hers in Bow churchyard.

'If you want to make inquiries about her, her mother's name is Mistress Alborow. The name of the daughter is Margaret Alborow, and she is not more than eighteen or nineteen. As for the money and plate, it is ready whenever she is to be married; as for the estates, I do not think these will be hers until after her mother's death; I do not know for certain, but you can find out by inquiring. As for her beauty, you can judge when you see her, if you take the trouble to do so; look at her hands particularly, because I am told that she is rather fat.'

Walter, aged about 23, was at Oxford, where he had been studying since 1473, and was now about to take his Bachelor of Arts degree. Margaret had high hopes of him, and wanted him to go into the church. She tried to get him a suitable benefice by writing to a influential church lawyer, Dr William Pickenham, but was told that Walter was not old enough and could not apply until he was in holy orders. She then thought of the law, which was the family profession, and his tutor at Oxford approved of this, suggesting that Walter took his degree at midsummer, spent the vacation at home, and went to the Inns in September. Walter did take his degree in June, and held the traditional feast afterwards, though, as he reported to Sir John 'I was promised venison for my feast by Lady Harcourt and another man as well, but they both let me down; but my guests said they were pleased with what they had, blessed be God. . .'

But soon after this, Walter was taken ill and brought home to Norfolk, where he died in early August. At the same time, old Agnes Paston, who was nearly eighty and who had settled in London five or six years earlier, died, as did Anne Yelverton's new-born child. It was a period when plague was rife, and when Sir John went back to London in October, he was worried about it, as he told Margaret and John.

'This is to let you know that I have been here at London a fortnight; for the first four days I was in great fear of the sickness, and also found my chamber and stuff not so clean as I thought it was, which worried me very much. . .'

He also complained – as always – of being very short of money, and was having great difficulty in borrowing any, all of which, he said, 'has made me more than half sick, so God help me.' His fears were all too justified: within a month he was dead. Apparently none of the family were with him, because he was buried in the White Friars Church at London, whereas the traditional burial place of the Pastons was at Bromholm. John III tried to get to London in time to bring his brother's body home, but was too late.

Whatever Sir John's failings as a businessman – and he had at least secured Caister for the family – he was certainly the most cultured member of the family, and his liking for the spendthrift, often dissolute world of Edward IV's court was undoubtedly a contribution to his financial problems. A most interesting list of books belonging to him survives, possibly drawn up after his death; the original is fragmentary, but we can fill in many of the missing words.

The inventory of the English Books of John Paston, made the fifth of November. . .

1. A book bought from my landlady at the George of the Death of Arthur beginning at Cassobelaunus, Warwick, King Richard Coeur de Lion, a chronicle up to Edward III

2. Item, a book of Troilus which William Bra . . . has had for nearly ten years and lent it to Daniel Wingfield, and I saw it there

3. A black book with the legend of Ladies, La Belle Dame Sans Mercy, the Parliament of Birds, the Temple of Glass, Palatyse and Scitacus, the Med. . ., the Green Knight

4. A printed book of *The Game and Play of Chess*

5. A book lent to Middleton: in it is Belle Dame Sans Mercy, the parliament of Birds, Ballad . . . of Guy and Colbronde, of the Goose, the. . ., the Dispute between Hope and Despair, . . . Merchants, the life of Saint Crispin

6. A red book that Percival Robsart gave me of the Meed of the Mars, the Lamentation. . . of Child Ypotis, A Prayer to the Vernicle . . . called the Abbey of the Holy Ghost

7. In quires, Tully de Senectute. . . of which there is only part clearly written
8. In quires, Tully or Scipio, de Amicitate, left with William Worcester
9. In quires, a book of the Policy of In. . .
10. In quires, a book de Sapiencia, whereon the Second person [of the Trinity] is likened to Sapiencia
11. A book de Othea, text and glosses, in quires
Memorandum, my old book of blazons of arms
The new book portrayed and blazoned
A copy of blazons of arms and. . . names to be found by letter
A book with arms portrayed, on paper
Memorandum, my book of Knighthood; in it. . .
of making knights, jousts, tournaments. . . , fighting in lists, places held by soldiers. . . and challenges, status of war and de Regimine. . .
A book of new statutes from Edward . . . the fourth

John III, who had worked hard enough over the family estates while his brother was alive, now found himself with the management of all of them, and with a new problem. Since his grandmother Agnes had died, in August, his uncle William was claiming the manors which had been her dowry long ago in 1420. By the terms of William I's will, however, Agnes had only a life interest, and they were to go to the heirs of both William I and Agnes. Agnes had lived with William II for some years, so he may have hoped to continue to hold the manors, which he looked after for her, after her death. The resulting quarrel is not well documented, but was certainly still going on well into the next decade, and the only indication we have that it was settled is that William II did not mention the disputed manors in his will in 1496.

After Sir John's death, the letters became very sparse; about five a year survive for the period 1480–5, including those letters to the Pastons from others. This is because John III was largely in Norfolk, administering his own estates, and there was therefore less need of letters than with the absentee Sir John. He was occasionally away for fairly long periods, but the fact that we have only three letters to him in London from Margery would imply that such journeys were the exception rather than the rule: Margery adds a postscript to one such letter in her own hand, having let Calle write the business part:

'Sir, I pray that if you stay in London long, you will be kind enough to send for me, for it seems a long time since I lay in your arms.'

Margery had evidently endeared herself to her mother-in-law, for when Margaret was thinking about her will, she asked her to see that John carried out the provisions of it, which provoked a protest from John that 'no ambassadors or negotiations are needed between you and me', though he was 'very glad that my wife is in any way favoured or trusted by you'. Margaret's health was failing. In February 1482 she made her will, but she actually died in November 1484. In her will she provided for a new aisle to be built at Mautby to house her tomb; this was duly built, but fell into ruin in the eighteenth century and was pulled down. She remembered all her family in the will; even Sir John's bastard daughter Constance and Margery Calle's children were left bequests. She named John as her executor.

John now found himself a substantial landowner, with his estates relatively secure, apart from the disputes with William II and the duke of Suffolk, which affected a few manors. But there were still political dangers. When, after a decade of peace in England, Edward IV died on April 9 1483, his heir, Edward V, was only twelve. There was immediate competition for control of the new king's person. On the one hand was the Woodville faction, relations of the queen mother, on the other supporters of Richard of Gloucester, the late king's brother. Richard of Gloucester quickly gained the upper hand, and was granted sweeping powers as protector, wider than any granted during Henry VI's minority. He was aware that there would be opposition, and, scenting a plot, had Lord Hastings executed without trial in June. As John Paston was well-known as a supporter of Hastings, having served with him at Calais as recently as May, he stood in danger, but was able to obtain a pardon in March 1484, by which time Richard had seized the throne. The Pastons' old enemy Sir John Howard was created duke of Norfolk in 1483, but past grievances seem to have been forgotten, and the two letters from him to John which survive are both friendly. The second was written in the second week of August 1485, when

Henry Tudor, earl of Richmond, had just landed in England to raise the standard of rebellion against Richard:

'*Well-beloved friend*, I commend myself to you. Please understand from this that the king's enemies have landed, and the king would have set out against them on Monday, but for the fact it was our Lady's Day*; but he is certainly going on Tuesday because a servant of mine brought me definite news.

'So please meet me at Bury, for by the grace of God I intend to stay at Bury for Tuesday night; and bring with you such a company of tall men as you can easily make up at my expense, as well as what you have promised the king; please arrange jackets of my livery for them, and I will repay you when we meet.'

John does not seem to have responded to the call. He returned to his earlier Lancastrian allegiance, and so avoided Howard's fate: the duke was killed at Bosworth Field a week later. John's fortunes prospered under the new regime. He was sheriff of Norfolk in the autumn of 1485, and two years later helped to put down Lambert Simnel's rebellion, when the Yorkists made a last attempt to regain power by pretending that Simnel was the earl of Warwick. The revolt was crushed at the battle of Stoke, and John was knighted for his services.

And on this auspicious note, with Sir John and Dame Margery Paston ensconced in their noble house at Caister, we take leave of the family.

---

* The Assumption of the Blessed Virgin (15 August).

EPILOGUE

In the more stable times of the Tudors, the Pastons flourished, both as country gentlemen and as courtiers. John III's son William took after his uncle, Sir John, and played a prominent part at Henry VIII's court; he was knighted at some time early in Henry VIII's reign, and although he played his part in local politics, as sheriff of Norfolk in 1517 and again in 1528, he was more often at the centre of affairs, attending the king at banquets or at the reception of the emperor Charles V on his visit to England in May 1520. The following month he was at Henry's famous meeting with Francis I at the Field of the Cloth of Gold. In 1524 he was delegated to meet the papal ambassador at Blackheath. At home in Norfolk, he was able to secure grants of part of the estate of the de la Poles, the dukes of Suffolk who had been among the family's arch-enemies, and his service both in peace in Norfolk and during Henry's Scottish wars secured more grants. Towards the end of his life he was one of the commissioners concerned in the suppression of the monasteries. He died in 1554 and was succeeded by his son Clement. It was Clement who built the house at Oxnead, the manor which William I had bought for Agnes in 1420, which became the family's seat instead of Caister Castle, now that comfort came before fortifications. Clement had no children, and was succeeded by his nephew William, who was knighted in 1578. He founded the grammar school at North Walsham, and also endowed Gonville and Caius College at Cambridge.

Under the Stuarts, the family reached its apogee, and their wealth became a local proverb: 'there was never a Paston poor, a Heydon a coward or a Cornwallis a fool.' Sir William's great-grandson, also called William, was born in 1610, the year of his great-grandfather's death. He was what the eighteenth century would have called a dilettante, interested in travel, literature, music and the arts, who formed a fine collection of paintings and sculpture. He was a friend of Thomas Browne and Thomas Fuller; and dictionaries and even cookery books were dedicated to him. In the civil war, he joined the Royalists in Holland but returned to make his peace at the cost of heavy fines to redeem the confiscation of his property. It was he who was forced to sell Caister Castle, by now in ruins, to a London merchant and the Paston fortunes never really recovered; but after his death in 1663 his son Sir Robert reaped the rewards of loyalty. Sir Robert became a close friend of Charles II, whom he entertained at Oxnead, and was created Viscount Yarmouth in 1673; he was also a gentleman of the privy chamber. On the intellectual side, he took up the new enthusiasm for scientific enquiry and became a founding fellow of the Royal Society in 1663. In 1679 he became earl of Yarmouth. But the family's glory was brief. His son William, the second earl, was treasurer of the household to James II, and after 1688 played little part in public life. He lived on until 1732, outliving all his sons, and gradually wasting his estates, until at his death the whole estate had to be sold and the title became extinct.

Until the second earl of Yarmouth's day, the Paston archives at Oxnead had remained intact, probably regarded as of little interest or value. But the antiquaries of the late seventeenth and early eighteenth centuries had begun to set store by such collections, and to pay good money for manuscripts. Accordingly, the second earl, needing cash, had sold part of the collection to the Norfolk antiquary Peter Le Neve; others were bought at his death by Francis Blomefield, author of a massive *History of Norfolk* which remains a standard reference work today. Blomefield's papers were dispersed at his death, and some eventually found their way to the Bodleian Library in Oxford. Le Neve's collections, which contained the most important papers, were preserved intact until 1771, but were then dispersed. Three years later John Fenn, another local antiquary, bought the Paston papers, and published them in two volumes in 1787, followed by three more volumes in 1789 and 1823. Normally this would have been the end of the story, particularly as the originals of the first two volumes were presented to the Royal Library when Fenn was knighted by George III for his work on the letters. But on the death of Fenn's nephew, Mr Frere, who had prepared the last volume for press after his uncle's death, all the manuscripts disappeared. By 1865 it was being suggested that the letters were no more than an ingenious hoax, since the originals had vanished so completely; but in that year the originals of the

last volume were found in the house of Mr Frere's son. Four years later the originals of volumes 3 and 4 of Fenn's edition were found in the house of Mr Frere's nephew. Yet the originals of the first two volumes which should have been in the Royal Library, were nowhere to be found, even though the Prince Consort himself had organised a search for them. They reappeared in 1890, at a house near Ipswich which belonged to the heirs of Dr Pretyman, Pitt's private secretary, who had arranged for Fenn to present them to the king, and had evidently borrowed them from the king soon afterwards. In 1933 they were sold to the British Museum, which had already acquired the other originals. No one would be more surprised than the Pastons to learn that it is on these papers, rather than on their political and social ambitions and achievements, that their fame now rests.